Insights *for a* Happier Life

Shortcuts for Creating Positive Changes One Moment at a Time

Steven Jay Fogel

FRESH RIVER PRESS

Fresh River Press
www.freshriverpress.com

Ordering Information

Quantity sales/orders for college textbook/course adoption use. Special discounts are available on quantity purchases by corporations, associations, and others. For details, contact the "Special Sales Department."

Orders by U.S. trade bookstores and wholesalers. Please contact BCH: (800) 431-1579 or visit www.bookch.com for details.

Printed in the United States of America

ISBN: 978-0-9845525-4-2

First Edition

19 18 17 16 15 10 9 8 7 6 5 4 3 2 1

PRAISE FOR STEVEN JAY FOGEL'S PREVIOUS BOOKS

"Wise advice, clearly presented, on how to lead a more fulfilling life."

—Helen Astin, PhD, and Alexander Astin, PhD, psychologists and Distinguished Professors Emeriti, UCLA Graduate School of Education and Information Studies

"In our most private moments, we all see the patterns in our lives that hold us back. But what we don't see clearly is how they were set in motion or how to go about changing things. Fogel lays out a blueprint for both—a map with easy-to-follow exercises designed to reset 'faulty writing' and create the potential to live healthier, more accepting, and more loving lives."

—Connell Cowan, PhD, coauthor of *Smart Women/Foolish Choices*

"How can you choose from the flurry of self-help books that attempt to help us navigate through our rapidly changing times? The beauty of *Your Mind Is What Your Brain Does for a Living* resides in its comprehensive appreciation of how we can control the timeless unconscious patterns of our childhoods right up to how the current contributions of the neurosciences can help us live more peacefully in the present."

—Fred M. Sander, MD, Clinical Associate Professor, Department of Psychiatry, Weill Cornell Medical College, and author of *Individual and Family Therapy*

"Among the many wise messages in *Your Mind Is What Your Brain Does for a Living* is that in order to nurture those you love, you must first nurture yourself. To learn how best to do that, turn to page 1 and keep reading."

—Ann Pleshette Murphy, parenting educator and author of *The 7 Stages of Motherhood*

"*Your Mind Is What Your Brain Does for a Living* serves as a practical bridge between understanding oneself and making the necessary changes for a more meaningful life. As a psychiatrist, I can say that it does so by providing building blocks for constructive self-awareness in a most accessible and organized fashion."

—Diane Weiss, MD

"*Your Mind Is What Your Brain Does for a Living* shows the reader how to live a successful and balanced life full of purpose. I am impressed that Fogel's positive and educated messaging will help many find their own roads to success."

—Tom Gores, Founder, Chairman, and CEO, Platinum Equity, LLC

"*Your Mind Is What Your Brain Does for a Living* presents any reader the direction and tools to climb out of the trap that keeps one from achieving a more fulfilling, transformative, and creative life."

—Roland A. Frauchiger, MA, MFT

"*My Mind Is Not Always My Friend* is a game changer. Fogel's insights will improve your life."

—Gray Davis, former Governor of California

"*My Mind Is Not Always My Friend* is both interesting and educational. It is a fast read and a profitable experience."

—Rabbi Isaiah Zeldin

CONTENTS

PREFACE

Why do situations and people upset us again and again? Why is our self-esteem fine one moment and in the next we are filled with feelings of inadequacy? What can we do to decrease frustration and stress? How can we create better relationships and experience more joy and fulfillment in our lives?

For the past three decades, my primary focus has been seeking answers to these questions, applying what I discovered, and sharing it with others.

In my first book, *The Yes-I-Can Guide to Mastering Real Estate* (Random House), I focused on teaching how to create wealth through real estate investment. I was gratified by the response I received from readers who felt it gave them the information they needed about successful investment in real estate, but I felt I had more to offer to help people achieve their goals, both personal and professional. Over the years I mentored many people, and the common thread I found was that I was helping them overcome emotional barriers to taking action so they could accomplish what they want out of life.

I wanted to share the lessons I learned about the psychology of achieving goals and also the biggest lesson I learned: that genuine success isn't just financial; it's learning to create a fulfilling life for ourselves. This led to my writing *My Mind Is Not Always My Friend: A Guide for How to Not Get in Your Own Way* (Fresh River, 2010) and *Your Mind Is What Your Brain Does for a Living: Learn How to Make It Work for You*

(Greenleaf Press, 2013), both coauthored with Mark Bruce Rosin, and now to my writing this book, *Insights for a Happier Life—One Moment at a Time.*

The phrase *one moment at a time* is vital to the insights I'm sharing because, as I've learned and as you'll see throughout this book, we create our lives one moment at a time, and every moment gives us an opportunity to create a new life experience.

We are reaction machines; we don't always have a choice about *what* happens to us, but we do have a choice about *how* we will react to it. No matter how we have reacted in the past, each new moment provides us the chance to let go of our old past-based thinking and react in new, more productive ways.

If we continue to think, act, and react in the same ways we always have, we will continue to feel exactly as we always have. But it doesn't have to be like that—we can learn to change. This is the subject of this book. It's based on my most popular blogs, especially those that people have found the most helpful, and my goal is for each chapter to offer insights that you can apply moment to moment and long term in order to support you in reducing stress and frustration and experiencing greater happiness.

Part I

MINDFUL MESSAGES ABOUT PERSONAL GROWTH

1

THE STORY OF ADAM AND EVE: A METAPHOR FOR ILLUMINATING THE WAY OUR MINDS WORK

The story of Adam and Eve is a great metaphor that can help us understand how our minds work.

When Adam and Eve lived in the Garden of Eden, they lived in a state of pure *being*, experiencing complete harmony without worry, fear, or the need to protect themselves or strategize for their survival. They were always in the now, the present, and would have stayed in that state for eternity were it not for the serpent's tempting them to disobey God by eating the forbidden fruit of *knowledge*.

As a result of eating the forbidden fruit, Adam and Eve were thrust out of Eden and became the first mortals. With *mortality* came the need to survive, and with the need to survive came *fear*—because all at once the world contained threats to the couple's survival. This meant that Adam and Eve each needed a mind capable of preemptive, defensive thinking—a mind able to anticipate, identify, and judge everything he or she encountered in the outside world, looking for potential dangers. This gave rise to the voice in their head.

Adam and Eve's peaceful and fearless days in the Garden of Eden without a worry or care were over. They now lived with the constant commentary of the often-critical voice in their head whose purpose was to help in their ongoing struggle for survival. From this point forward, harmony became a touch-and-go experience.

HOW OUR MINDS WORK TODAY

As Adam and Eve's metaphorical descendants, we have inherited the same judging mind that scans and evaluates everyone and everything as it surveys the horizon for threats and tells us what to think and to feel about ourselves and the world outside us. The mind has become our central command center. Its *machinery*—the term I use for the workings of the mind when it's on automatic pilot—is still preoccupied with scanning and evaluating, speaking to us through the voice in our head.

It's like constantly hearing the voice of a GPS, just like the device in our cars, except instead of telling us "Turn left in a quarter of a mile and you will arrive at your destination," it tells us what to think and how to act and feel. The machinery that triggers the voice is still programmed to attempt to ensure our survival, whether it's telling us how we should flirt with someone we're attracted to or how to talk a traffic officer out of giving us a ticket when he just pulled us over for a rolling stop.

STAYING IN THE TRIBE

There's another important aspect to the way our minds work when we're on automatic pilot. To understand it, let's look back at our cave-dwelling ancestors who were hunter-gatherers living in tribes in the era of woolly mammoths. Back then,

humans needed to live in tribes to survive, and they knew that being shunned by the tribe was a probable death sentence. As a result, the human mind became programmed with techniques designed to keep one's place in the tribe.

Much time has passed since then, but our machinery is still programmed the same way. We can still experience the possibility of being rejected or disapproved of by others as if it's a matter of life and death, and often we react to such perceived threats in unnecessary ways that are inappropriate and unproductive, creating collateral damage to our relationships.

Put simply, our mind can, and often does, mistakenly experience a situation that we find ourselves in as a matter of life and death when it isn't that at all. When this happens, unless we stop ourselves and recognize that our mind's interpretation is incorrect, we will react automatically, and the results will be destructive.

HOW OUR MIND'S PROGRAMMING IS FORMED

Starting in childhood, each of us develops our own unique ways of thinking and acting that, by the time we're adults, become our programmed strategies to cope in the world. This programming is unique to each individual because it's always a result of our experiences growing up, especially traumatic experiences. I refer to this programming as our *default programming.* I think of our default programming as the "software" for our mind's machinery.

With this programming, our mind on automatic pilot instantly reacts to events in the present by scanning and evaluating them, and if it judges an event in the present to be similar to an event in the past that it perceived as a threat, it tells us to react to the new event just as we did to the previous event.

When we're on automatic pilot, we don't question the voice in our head telling us "This is how it is and this is what you should do." But what the voice in our head is telling us is just the reaction of our default programming—and it can be wrong because *when we're on automatic pilot, we are not really in the present; we are simply repeating behaviors that our mind believes worked for us in the past.* This keeps us in the past instead of in the present. We may believe that we're acting in a way that is best for us, but we may actually be acting in a way that's self-defeating.

WHAT MINDFULNESS IS AND HOW IT HELPS US

Recognizing that our mind on automatic pilot may be mistaken about what it judges to be a threat and how we should react to it is the first step toward *mindfulness.* Mindfulness is focusing on the present with intent, being in the present instead of allowing ourselves to be run on automatic pilot by our past-based default programming.

Being mindful allows us to let go of the interpretations and judgments that pass through our mind and to actually experience what is happening in the here and now. *Being mindful allows us to run our programming instead of letting our programming run us.*

Learning how to be mindful is the greatest gift you can give to yourself. It's a subject I will return to again and again in this book because it's so vital.

2

MEMORIES

I've come to look at my memories differently than I used to. I used to think of my memories as being precise and stable, but I now know this isn't true and I have less trust in their accuracy. I now understand that over time they can change. I came to this understanding about memories years ago when I discovered that if I leave a contract in a drawer unread for twelve months, God will play a practical joke and change the words.

This lesson was hard and expensive. I'm in the real-estate ownership business, which can be very litigious. We own many multitenant properties with thousands of leases, many of which were the result of both emotionally spirited and hard-fought negotiations.

Occasionally there will be a contentious dispute, and one side or the other will eventually say "Sue the bastards!" I'll remember vividly what the contract says and get upset with the other party, knowing I'm in the right, and the war will be on. Then I'll reread the contract and be shocked to see it doesn't say what it said when I signed it! Or at least it doesn't say what I remembered that it said.

A second example of memories changing comes from having the blessing of spending the last four years living with my ninety-six-year-old mother. It's given me the opportunity to see how in her very late years her memories of a tormented childhood have shifted into her seeing her tormentors as warm and loving instead of as parents who had filled her with terror.

Until recently, my mother talked about her childhood as one with a mother who showed little affection and who often cut people out of her life if she had a disagreement with them and a father who was too passive. I find myself amused because in old age my mother prefers to remember both her parents as being sweet, kind, and loving.

How is it that my mind can vividly remember the details of a contract only to let time lapse, but when I reread it, I discover that the contract says entirely different things? How is it that my mother goes almost a whole lifetime angry at and afraid of her mother who's been dead for years, and all of a sudden she turns her mother into a saint? These examples show that memories aren't always accurate and, in fact, may change as time goes by.

WHAT SCIENTISTS HAVE DISCOVERED ABOUT MEMORIES

I read an article in *Wired* magazine that explained why our memories can change over time. Most of us think that our important memories exist in a fixed way, stored in our brain like films or videos, which always replay the same way. But clearly, this belief is inaccurate. Here's why.

Scientists have discovered that memories are formed through neural connections and chemicals, and that in the act of remembering an event, a memory is actually reconstituted or reassembled. Different parts of the memory of that event—the visual images, the sounds, the emotions, all the various aspects of the memory—are stored in different parts of the brain, and when we recall the event, the brain rebuilds the memory by combining all its different aspects. And that memory may be remembered slightly differently, depending on how we're feeling at the moment we reassemble it.[1]

Let's say you're remembering a dinner with your significant other. If you're hungry when you remember the evening, you may have a more vivid memory of the food. If you're feeling loving while recalling the incident, you may see the memory through a more loving lens. If you're feeling anxious about your relationship, you may remember things that would support your feeling anxious now. The point is that the emotions you feel in the present moment may affect or reshape how you remember past events.

OTHER FACTORS THAT CAN INFLUENCE OUR MEMORIES

New information or knowledge can also change a memory. Let's say you notice a family dealing with an angry child who is having a tantrum. Your first reaction is thinking what a brat the child is and that the parents should have more control over him. Later you learn that the child is autistic, so your memory of the incident changes, and by feeling compassion for the child and parents when you remember the event, you realize that the parents were doing the best they could.

New circumstances in the present can change memories of the past, too. I've known people who endured years in an unhappy marriage with a difficult spouse and who remember only good things about their marriage once the spouse has died.

It's human nature to recall an event the way we want to see it. On the other hand, it's also a common tendency to convert painful memories into more harmonious memories by forgiving grievances or painting over events with brighter colors than were actually there or by focusing on different aspects of the event than those that were prominent to us during the time of the event.

REINTERPRETING MEMORIES OF CHILDHOOD

Years of therapy have helped me shift many of my childhood memories. For example, I used to believe that I was forced to be "the man of the family" after my father died, even though I was only eleven years old, because my mother was too unstable to be depended on. I believed that this responsibility robbed me of my childhood by "parentifying" me long before I reached adulthood. I spent most of my thirties and forties becoming (silently) angry at my mother for not being a better mother and for letting me take responsibility that I wasn't equipped for.

Over time I've come to see my mother differently, from the perspective of her *wiring*. For all of us, the wiring or neural circuitry—the connections between nerve cells—in our brain and throughout our body is formed in part by our genes and in part by the interplay between our genes and our experiences in the world. This wiring enables the biological functions that we need to live, such as breathing and the beating of our hearts, and it enables us to act and react. Our individual wiring is unique to each of us, which explains why we act and react in the particular ways we do. Thus, our wiring is the physiological basis for how our machinery and programming control our behavior when we're on automatic pilot.

Seeing my mother from the perspective of her wiring, I realized that the traumatic experiences she had had resulted in her being emotionally fragile. I also came to realize that she had never *asked* me to take care of her; I had taken on the job because I didn't trust her stability. It was my doing, believing that the only way I could survive was to take care of her and to have no conflicting needs of my own. Interpreting the situation with my own particular programming, I'd volunteered to be "parentified."

This change of understanding did not take away the painful effects of having lost my childhood at age eleven—it didn't make my childhood experience less of a challenge for me—but it did help me to let go of my anger and allow me to heal and forgive. My anger transformed into compassion.

I still had scars, but I saw the scars differently. And the new information I had about how we are wired and our potential for change helped me see that, through mindfulness—paying attention to the present instead of letting my programming from the past run me—I could transform myself and have a more fulfilling life.

A friend shared a similar experience of how additional knowledge about his father reshaped his memories of him. While my friend was growing up, his father, who was angry and controlling, often lost his temper and hit my friend, which had made my friend hate him. Years later, my friend learned that part of his father's issues stemmed from what had happened to him earlier in life.

When my friend's father was six years old, he had found his own father's body after his father had committed suicide. This had a profound negative effect on my friend's father because, besides losing his own father, he was raised by his angry, abusive older brother because his mother had to work full time. My friend's father's wiring that resulted from his own childhood caused him to copy his brother's parenting style in parenting my friend. Learning this new family history allowed my friend to heal and have more compassion for his father.

As with me, my friend's scars are still there, but he sees the scars a different way and is committed to fulfilling his potential to change and to grow in the present.

3

WHAT IS A COMPLEX—AND WHY DOES IT HELP TO KNOW ABOUT COMPLEXES?

Pioneer psychoanalyst Carl Jung coined the word *complex* to describe the "minipersonalities" that we form unconsciously in reaction to traumatic relationships and experiences in our early lives.[1]

If, for example, we have a traumatic relationship with our father or mother, we develop a father or a mother complex, which may cause us to feel awful and act inappropriately—or to freeze up and not act at all—when we encounter someone that our programming interprets as being similar to our parent.

Jung believed that even if our parents were very nurturing, we will still have a mother complex or a father complex to at least a small degree because there are certain areas in which even a good parent does not respond with attunement to a child's needs, and the child may experience this as traumatic.

A common type of father or mother complex (because it can be created by experiences with either parent) is a "people pleasing" complex. A typical example of this is someone's constantly apologizing for everything he or she does or says. This kind of complex generally comes from having a parent who was tyrannical, who frightened the child, and who made the child feel inadequate or wrong.

OTHER TYPES OF MOTHER AND FATHER COMPLEXES

A boy with a controlling mother can grow up into a man with a mother complex that makes him attracted to controlling women, even though he may resent them for being controlling or for trying to control him. Similarly, a girl with a father who is controlling can grow into a woman who is attracted to men like her father, even though she may resent their desire to control her. The familiarity of the controlling behavior is part of what attracts people with these types of complexes to partners who are like their controlling parent.

WHAT HAPPENS WHEN WE'RE IN A COMPLEX—AND WHAT TO DO ABOUT IT

When we're in a complex—that is, when we're on automatic pilot and experiencing the effects of the complex—the mini-personality has its own preprogrammed point of view, and the *amygdala*—the part of the brain that reacts emotionally with a fight-or-flight response—runs the show. When the amygdala is running the show, it bypasses the executive functions that, if we are functioning in a healthy manner, can modulate our emotional reactions and that enable rational thought. In this nonreasoning state, people we encounter tend to be, in our perceptions, heroes or villains, sinners or saints, all good or all bad, and we feel awful. The lesson to be learned is never trust your automatic reactions while you're in a complex because while you're in a complex, you're not thinking correctly. Never make a decision when you're in a complex!

The solution is to be mindful, which allows you to separate your perceptions or interpretations from the reality of what is happening. When you're mindful, you are able to see a person for who he or she is as opposed to your interpretations of who that person is. With mindfulness, you can remind yourself that you are an adult, no longer a child, and that the person you are encountering is not your parent—and, indeed, may not even possess the qualities that your programming is interpreting that person as having. When and only when you've made this shift and are able to get out of the complex are you prepared to act appropriately and responsibly—responsibly to your adult self.[2]

4

WHAT TO DO IF YOU'RE VERY SELF-CRITICAL

A friend of mine told me that she often found herself ruminating about the mistakes she feels she made parenting her children when they were young, even though she thinks her adult children are wonderful people. The fact that she's proud of them now, that she's apologized to her children for what she considers her mistakes, and that they love her didn't stop her self-criticism or alleviate the guilt she felt.

Like my friend, I have a very vocal inner self-critic that, if I allow it to, will magnify the negatives, minimize the positives, and often see future possibilities through a filter of pessimism, which tends to temporarily blind me to all that is truly possible.

I want to clarify: by inner self-critic, I'm not talking about mindfully realizing that we've done or said something inappropriate or harmful, taking responsibility for it, apologizing, and making amends; I'm talking about having an inner self-critic that continually dwells on what it judges to be our faults, beats ourselves up for them, and creates in us a state of low self-esteem.

I've done a lot of work over the years to temper my inner self-critic—through a process of mindfully looking at what this inner critic has to say and learning to disempower it. I've found that the first step to disempowering our inner self-critic is to understand what created it.

HOW OUR INNER CRITIC IS FORMED

Our inner critic is always past based—it uses our past experiences and the reactions and interpretations we had of them to create the programming for the self-critical commentary we hear as adults. We received most of those initial negative learning experiences as children, usually from our parents, other caretakers, or siblings.

When we received criticism, we internalized it, and it still lives as a voice in our head, which will continue to echo the same judgments every time a new event appears that the mind associates with a past event. For example, if as kids we were regularly told that we were wrong or not good enough by our parents, siblings, or caretakers, then, as adults, if we aren't mindful, we will allow our inner self-critic to operate on automatic pilot and repeat the same kinds of critical messages when we are unsure about ourselves.

A child's inner self-critic can be vicious. Consider, for instance, how common it is for a child to mistakenly blame himself or herself for a parent's death or a divorce even though the child bears no responsibility for it.

Children who experience feeling that it's their fault that their parents divorced, for example, may grow into adults who perpetually feel that they're not good enough—very often blaming themselves when something goes wrong. This phenomenon is similar to how abused children continue to feel unworthy because on some level they blame themselves for their abuse rather than holding the perpetrator accountable.

This pattern of self-blame will perpetuate into adulthood where, when we're on automatic pilot, we unconsciously allow our inner self-critic to attach those old, false feelings of unworthiness to current situations in which we also feel unworthy and responsible.

DISEMPOWERING OUR INNER SELF-CRITIC

Once we understand how our inner self-critic is created and perpetuated, we need to disempower it by mindfully voicing to ourselves this simple truth: *my inner self-critic is not me; it's not an appropriate, productive part of my thought process; it's just old pain, developed in childhood, causing a false sense of unworthiness in the present.*

By using this mindful approach, I am able to hear the self-criticism and simply tell myself, "It's just my old programming," and let the thoughts pass by like clouds floating through the sky rather than holding on to the criticism as if it were the truth. The result for me is less pain and a greater ability to live in the present where good things are possible and I can feel good about myself.

Several months ago, I shared this with my friend. A few weeks later she told me that, reflecting mindfully on what caused her to be so self-critical, she realized that her vocal self-critic was formed in childhood when her judgmental mother constantly criticized her. By mindfully reminding herself that her self-criticism is part of this old programming, she is able to stop ruminating, let go of that habit of magnifying her flaws as a parent, and instead of barraging herself with criticism, experience her children's love and appreciation of her.

5

EMBRACE YOUR DARK SIDE

Have you ever spent time with someone and come away feeling upset, thinking she was conceited, arrogant, or aggressive or behaving in some other way you judged to be wrong? Has another person ever asked you why you were so angry and you denied that you were—only to have that person show you how angry your words and tone of voice were? What do these experiences have in common? They're both hidden gifts with the power to introduce you to aspects of your dark side.

Your reaction of being upset by another person's behavior and your blindness to your own anger have their roots in the part of your unconscious mind that psychoanalyst Carl Jung called your *dark side* or *personal unconscious.*

Your conscious mind—what you think of as *I* or *me*—contains all the parts of yourself—including your actions, words, thoughts, memories, and feelings, that you're aware of. Your dark side contains the specific parts of yourself that your conscious mind finds intolerable because they clash with your pictures of yourself and judges them as unacceptable or bad. In other words, what your conscious mind cannot own is banished to your dark side.

WHY IT'S IMPORTANT TO KNOW ABOUT YOUR DARK SIDE

Although your conscious mind represses the emotions, thoughts, and memories it judges as bad or finds too difficult or painful to accept, these feelings, thoughts, and memories do not go away; they live in the dark side and create self-defeating patterns of behavior—unconscious ways of acting that work against your conscious goals. *Traits that remain hidden in your dark side still sabotage your life.*

CLUES TO THE TRAITS IN YOUR DARK SIDE

When another person's actions upset you, it may be because you are reacting to something in your dark side that you're unaware of and that your conscious mind considers unacceptable.

For example, if your conscious mind equates expressing pride in your accomplishments with being boastful and vain, you may be upset when another person talks with pride about his accomplishments and brand him as conceited and arrogant. This doesn't necessarily mean he is conceited and arrogant; it just means an old message in your conscious mind says it's bad to express pride in yourself. In this case, you judge the other person because of your own issues about showing pride. In fact, you may be so self-critical when it comes to expressing pride that you cannot allow yourself to express any pride in your accomplishments!

If you have negative judgments about asking for what you want, you might be upset when someone else asks for what she wants and judge her negatively as aggressive. Again, this is due to old messages in your programming. The other person may simply be freer than you in expressing herself, and that's what is upsetting you. Your conscious mind doesn't believe that you should have permission to express yourself as freely.

If you believe anger is an unacceptable emotion, your anger gets banished to your dark side, where it stays hidden and you can't consciously and appropriately express it. Unfortunately you're stuck—because your anger will still come out, but it will come out inappropriately. This is why, in the example I gave above, someone can act angrily and be completely unaware of it until someone points it out; the anger that explodes without the person being aware of it has come from the dark side.

HOW TO BECOME AWARE OF YOUR DARK SIDE—AND WHY IT'S VITAL TO DO SO

According to Jungian therapist Leana Melat, PhD, Jung observed that the less conscious you are of your dark side, the blacker and denser it becomes.[1] As the examples illustrate, this lack of awareness creates frustration, stress, and confusion. When you act unconsciously, others are likely to react to you—and you're likely to react to them—in ways you don't quite understand. As long as parts of yourself are hidden in your dark side, you will deprive yourself of self-knowledge, self-expression, and the ability to feel your appropriate feelings.

That's why it's so important to become aware of those parts of yourself that you've banished to your dark side and to embrace them. There are three major ways to accomplish this:

- Look mindfully at your interactions with others to see what they tell you about your behavior. If you habitually react negatively to people who act in a certain way that you deem to be wrong—for example, boastful or aggressive—ask yourself if it's because you would like to act in that way yourself but have internalized the message that it's bad.

- Ask yourself if other people react to you in ways that surprise you—and that you're tempted to deny. What do these reactions tell you about how you're acting that you've been unaware of?
- Look at your dreams. Keep a dream journal. Dreams can tell you a lot about what you're hiding from yourself.

Embracing your dark side—integrating the traits that you've unconsciously banished there and beginning to work consciously and constructively with them—helps you live a happier, more fulfilling life. As Jung emphasized, it helps you become whole and authentic; it vitalizes your personality and allows your normal instincts, appropriate reactions, realistic insights, and creative impulses to take their natural place in your behavior. By embracing your dark side, Jung remarked, the carbon turns into a diamond.[2]

6

A LIFE LESSON THAT WORKS

A long time ago I learned that if you tell the truth and keep your agreements, life will turn out perfectly; the bad news is that *perfectly* may not fit your picture.

TELLING THE TRUTH AND KEEPING OUR AGREEMENTS

"Tell the truth" is easy to understand. It simply means to communicate honestly—about yourself, your feelings, your needs, whatever situation you're discussing—without lies or even what we might think of as white lies or little fibs.

"Keep your agreements" is also easy to understand. It comes down to keeping your word, doing what you said you would do.

To use a minor example, if you agree to be at a certain place at a certain time and you're there when you say you will be, you're keeping your agreement. When you do this consistently, people know they can depend on your word. On the other hand, if you're often late, you foster negative feelings, and people may feel that you're not to be trusted, at least not in that area. At another level, if you're in a monogamous relationship and you're faithful, you're keeping your word; whereas if you're unfaithful, you're not acting with integrity, which is going to cause problems.

Every time we break an agreement, we create upset for ourselves and others. The more we break our agreements with other people, the less they trust us. Internally it works the same way: if we break agreements with ourselves, we lose self-trust, turning our intentions into hollow words. Essentially, keeping our agreements is about having integrity. Remember, that means keeping our word to ourselves as well as to others.

WHAT CAN HAPPEN TO TELLING THE TRUTH WHEN WE'RE ON AUTOMATIC PILOT

I get into the most trouble about telling the truth when I'm acting on automatic pilot. When I speak without mindfulness, my response can lack integrity. One of my biggest traps lies in my reluctance to say no to people I care about out of fear that my declining will lead to their abandoning me.

If, for example, a friend asks, "Can I stay with you for a while?" and I know I don't want to give up my privacy for that long and that the visit would create a strain, it's important for me to tell the truth. If I allow my default programming to run me and I say yes because I don't have the guts to say no, I'm responding without integrity simply to avoid friction in the relationship.

When we lie, we are dishonoring ourselves and making it impossible to satisfy our desires and needs. Take our basic need for intimacy, for instance. If we're in a relationship and want more intimacy than our partner is offering and we don't tell the truth about it, our partner will think we're satisfied, and we run the risk of never having our desires and needs met.

We may rationalize that our need for intimacy and connection isn't really there, but it is. When we share our feelings with our partner, we are being true to ourselves, and we will get the perfect result. If the result is more connection with our partner, then it fits our picture of perfect. If the result is a breakup, it's perfect, too, even though it doesn't fit our picture because of the pain we feel losing the relationship as we desire it to be. It will be perfect, however, because we'll be free to get the nurturing we need from someone else. So, again, the result is perfect, even if it doesn't fit our picture.

WHAT DOES PERFECT MEAN?

I've come to understand that perfect simply means *as it is*. Indeed, the Merriam-Webster dictionary tells us that perfect means "satisfying all requirements: accurate."[1] Knowing that *what is* is simply *as it is* satisfies all requirements of the current circumstance; it is accurate.

When we repress our truth, we cannot possibly be fulfilled: whereas when we put our needs on the table and let go of fear, whatever happens is a response to who we really are, and that's perfect.

THE CHOICES WE HAVE FOR DEALING WITH ANY SITUATION

Once we know the reality of a situation, we always have three choices:

- Accept the situation fully (which I call Door 1).
- Change the situation (Door 2).
- Leave the situation (Door 3).

When we tell the truth and keep our agreements, we are living mindfully instead of letting our default programming run us on automatic pilot. When we live this way, we are living with integrity and are open to new possibilities.

7

SIX STEPS FOR SELF-TRANSFORMATION

Self-transformation is self-motivated change from within that increases your ability to accomplish your goals. It comes from shifting your perception, realizing that whatever situation you are in, you are responsible for your own experience of stress, frustration, and unhappiness. In other words, by transforming yourself, you'll also transform your experience of that situation.

If you find yourself unhappy because you're acting in a way that creates frustration and stress in any area of your life—for example, if you habitually refrain from being assertive, even though doing so is at your own expense—it's an opportunity for you to engage in self-transformation. Self-transformation involves six steps.

STEP 1: DECIDE THAT YOU WANT TO TRANSFORM YOURSELF AND COMMIT TO THE PROCESS

Motivation is a key to self-transformation. We tend to resist change because change is scary. Change means giving up familiar ways and entering unknown territory. Even if the old ways are painful and produce less-than-stellar results, we tend to stick with them because we know we can exist with that pain. It is *familiar pain*, and consciously or unconsciously we fear that *unfamiliar pain* will be worse. Generally, we make the decision to transform ourselves only when something in our lives is going so badly that we don't want to put up with it anymore.

To shift your perception, you need to look within instead of blaming external circumstances for your dissatisfaction. Acknowledge that something you're doing is contributing to the experiences you dislike and that you want to change it to produce better results. This means recognizing that if you want your present to be different from your past, *you* have to be different from how you've been up to now. One of the definitions of insanity is doing the same thing over and over always expecting a different result.

For example, let's say that in reading the chapter "Embrace Your Dark Side," you realized that you tend to judge other people as bad or wrong when you perceive them as being too aggressive. Reflecting on this mindfully, you realize that you have a pattern of not being assertive enough in stating your opinions or needs, even in your closest relationships. Once you've decided that you'd like to be more assertive, you've taken the first step in transforming yourself.

STEP 2: LOOK AT YOUR PAST AND IDENTIFY THE DYSFUNCTIONAL PATTERNS THAT HAVE BEEN DETERMINING YOUR ACTIONS AND EXPERIENCES UP TO NOW

This step requires learning how your mind works.

As I've discussed, essentially the mind hasn't changed much since the days of hunting and gathering. It still operates like our ancestors' minds did thousands of years ago: it interprets everything that happens, and based on those interpretations, it invents tactics intended to help us survive.

It doesn't matter whether you're facing an important meeting or a woolly mammoth from prehistoric times, your mind is always looking for ways to survive anything it perceives as a threat to your survival—which might be as minor as somebody's dirty look or a comment the mind interprets as an insult. Remember, the mind bases its survival strategies on what it believes worked in past situations. It does this automatically, without your conscious awareness, and when your mind is on automatic pilot, your machinery runs you with the mental software I call your *default programming*.

To transform yourself, you must become aware of your individual programming, the voice in your head that tells you how to act and react to everything you encounter. The process of self-transformation requires you to monitor that voice—to realize that the voice isn't you, it's just part of you, and it's not your boss. Self-transformation requires learning to question the mind's perceptions and interpretations. When your mind is acting automatically—as it does most of the time—it can give you good or bad advice.

Self-transformation requires letting go of past-based patterns that no longer work but that are still influencing how you think and act. And this means looking at your past to see how it has influenced the way you have thought and acted up to now.

Continuing with the example of wanting to be more assertive, mindfully reflect on your past to see when and how you first started behaving in a nonassertive way. Perhaps while you were growing up you felt that one or both of your parents ignored, criticized, or got angry at you when you spoke up for yourself, so you developed the belief that not asserting yourself was the best policy, and this developed into a pattern with other people as well. Or perhaps one or both of your parents were passive, nonassertive people, and you've copied their behavior and acted the same way.

STEP 3: IDENTIFY YOUR OLD ORGANIZING PRINCIPLES

All of us have conscious and unconscious beliefs that we hold as facts instead of realizing that they're only perceptions based on feelings. These beliefs, which come from our past experiences, have been dictating how we act. I call these mistaken beliefs that we hold as facts our *Organizing Principles.*

An Organizing Principle that could underlie the behavior of not asserting yourself is, "The best way to keep relationships peaceful is to keep my opinions and needs to myself."

STEP 4: CREATE NEW GUIDING PRINCIPLES

To transform yourself, you have to replace your old dysfunctional principles with new positive principles that will bring you from the past into the present. This will open you up to the possibility of getting what you want—new and more fulfilling experiences. I call these new principles *Guiding Principles.*

A Guiding Principle to support becoming more assertive is, "I have the right to express my opinions and needs, and any person worth being close to will support me in being authentically myself and fully self-expressed."

STEP 5: INTERRUPT YOUR MENTAL MACHINERY BY OBSERVING YOUR OLD ORGANIZING PRINCIPLES, AND INSTEAD OF USING OLD ORGANIZING PRINCIPLES, MINDFULLY SUBSTITUTE YOUR NEW GUIDING PRINCIPLES

Feeling defensive, upset, angry, anxious, or frustrated is a clue that the voice in your head is reacting to your situation based on your old Organizing Principles. When any of these feelings come up, know that you can choose to stop reacting automatically and instead make the mindful choice to use your new Guiding Principles.

With the example of being nonassertive, if you find yourself feeling upset in a relationship because you're holding back what you think and feel—not expressing who you truly are—it's a signal that you are not asserting yourself by being fully self-expressed, and that you need to remind yourself of your new Guiding Principle that will help you let go of this dysfunctional behavior.

STEP 6: LIVE FEARLESSLY

Self-transformation comes from being courageous. You have to let go of past conditioning and proceed into unknown territory, facing fears and not giving in to them. *Living fearlessly doesn't mean you won't have fears; it means acknowledging your fears and moving ahead anyway.* Instead of letting your fears keep you in the past, you have to apply what you've learned about yourself, your default programming, and how to interrupt that programming, so that you'll move into the present, where anything is possible. This is the essence of self-transformation.

8

THOUGHTS ABOUT THE STATUE OF BUDDHA

I have a huge statue of Buddha (about five feet tall and 800 pounds) in my front garden. It's unique, inspiring, and pleasing, and even a glance reassures me that everything's going to be okay in a larger sense.

The feeling reminds me of when my children were little and sharing their fears. We'd discuss them, and I'd say "it would be okay," and they would trust me and let go of the issue. Seeing the Buddha triggers that kind of response in me, as if someone I trust is telling me, "It's going to be okay." But what does okay mean?

WHAT CAUSES US TO BECOME UPSET?

There are three things that always result in upsets. They are attachment to

1. Unfulfilled expectations
2. Thwarted intentions
3. Incomplete communications

Whenever I'm agitated, it's because I can't get something I'm attached to wanting (in other words, I have an unfulfilled expectation or thwarted intention) or because my words or deeds are ignored (an incomplete communication).

Hence, Buddha's huge "aha" realization—that all human suffering comes from our attachment to people, things, or desires. The default belief system of our machinery includes the belief that we must have *it*—whatever it is that we're attached to—in order to survive.

Attachment is a point of view in our machinery's programming. It's as if the machinery has an innate gravitational pull to our attachments. These attachments are embedded in our minds as if what we're telling ourselves is true when it's only a story that we told ourselves. We refuse to see it as a story; however, because we believe that it's both real and the truth.

About 2,500 years ago, the Buddha said we are each a self-contained, self-generating universe, connected to all things and people. To remember this and fight the tendency toward attachment from my machinery, I practice mindfulness: I focus on the present, let go of the voice in my head, and remind myself that life works perfectly and I don't have to do anything to it.

When people ask me, "How are you?" I tell them, "I am the perfect me." This is very similar to what my late friend Dennis Rosoff, a preeminent Beverly Hills furrier, once said when he looked at my dog: "You know, Steven, that dog's coat is a perfect fit." I remind myself that I am perfect as we all are perfect, in the same way that every furry animal has a coat with a perfect fit.

NO ATTACHMENT NECESSARY

As you know, one of my mantras is "Life works perfectly; you don't have to do a thing to it." It means that whatever is happening, life has brought me the Universe's perfect, logical consequence for the string of events and experiences that led up to this moment.

I remind myself that yes, it is perfect, but often perfect does not fit my picture—which is why it's important to remember that at this moment I also have the ability to make mindful choices that can change my experience.

When our attachment to our pictures is so strong that it seems as if we're not going to get what we believe we need, our machinery has a tendency to go out of whack as if something is wrong. We become activated, which creates distorted feelings that get in the way of acting mindfully and of recognizing the Universe's perfection.

Seeing the image of the Buddha reminds me that the Universe is perfect and if I'm upset because it doesn't seem perfect, I'm letting my machinery run me and I'm reacting because I'm attached to my idea of what's perfect. If I'm mindful, I will see the perfection of the Universe, and I will know with my inner knowing that everything is, indeed, okay.

Pause Your Machinery

Here and at the end of the five sections that follow, I'll ask you to stop and take a moment to pause your machinery. The concepts and techniques in this book will help you learn mindfulness, and these brief written exercises will give you the opportunity to rest, step outside of the pattern of passive reading, and bring yourself into the present moment to reflect and apply the information to your life. Keep your written answers because they will be valuable for you to review later and to refer to in doing subsequent exercises.

You may want to use a new notebook or open a computer file so you can keep all your responses together in one place. Even if you do only some of these exercises and read the rest but don't do them right away, just pausing your machinery and reflecting mindfully on the instructions—particularly the questions I ask you to ask yourself—is a powerful tool that engages you in the process of being mindful.

- Take out your notebook (or open a new computer file) and describe in writing two or three areas of your life where you feel you've been operating on automatic pilot and would benefit from being more mindful. Describe what happens, how you act, and how you feel in these areas when you allow your default programming to run you, and then describe how being mindful will help you decrease stress and frustration and increase fulfillment.
- List the names of one or more people who have been close to you that you feel have hurt you. Describe what it is about how they have acted that has hurt you. Ask yourself what may have influenced their behavior. Does

looking at them from this perspective help you to see and understand them more clearly? Does it change your feelings about them in any way? If so, describe how your feelings have changed.

- If you feel you have a mother or father complex, reflect mindfully on your childhood and describe how this complex developed. Describe what type of person generally sets you off into a complex. Describe how you feel and how you act when you're in a complex. Describe the steps you'll take the next time you're in a complex to become mindful and disengage from it.
- If you are self-critical, reflect on your growing up and see if one or both of your parents was very critical of you (and possibly himself or herself, too). If this was the case, describe the kinds of criticism you received. Can you see the relationship between this criticism and how you criticize yourself now? What you've just described is the development and some of the content of your default programming, which runs you when you're on automatic pilot. Now describe the steps you'll take to be mindful and let go of this judgmental criticism.
- Ask yourself if there is a particular type of person whom you find annoying or who triggers an angry reaction in you. If so, what about the person cues this response? Do you feel that deep down you may have some of the same deeply rooted personality characteristics that you've hidden in your subconscious or dark side because you think they're wrong or bad? Now describe where you think this judgment came from.

- Describe one or two incidents in the last few weeks that upset you. Reflecting mindfully on the incidents, describe whether they resulted from unfulfilled expectations, thwarted intentions, or undelivered communications.

Part II

EXPANDING YOUR LIFE BY OPENING YOURSELF TO NEW POSSIBILITIES

9

POSSIBILITY—PART I

Possibility—we're so used to the word that we take it for granted. But for me, possibility isn't just a word; it's a concept, a philosophy, a way of life. And it's something I had to learn and I still have to be mindful of to make sure I put it into practice. Here's what I mean.

Webster's New World College Dictionary defines *possibility* as "the quality or condition of being possible," and it defines *possible* as something "that can be; capable of existing."[1] Especially in difficult times like these, it's important to approach the world with the attitude that what you want can be, that it is capable of existing.

When you approach life from an attitude of possibility, you open the door to new, uncharted territory, and that is the land of miracles. This is why understanding possibility is so vital.

HOW WE BENEFIT FROM AN ATTITUDE OF POSSIBILITY

I'm not saying that an attitude of possibility has some kind of secret mystical power to help us achieve our goals; I'm saying something much more concrete—that an attitude of possibility affects our behavior, creating strength and options to achieve our goals.

Our views about what's happening in the present and what will happen in the future are determined by our past experiences and our conscious and unconscious interpretations of them. Whether we realize it or not, until we consider possibility with mindful awareness—an intentional focus on the here and now—we are stuck with the judgments the voice in our head may be making. To approach life with an attitude of possibility, we have to actually be in the present—experiencing what is right here right now—and not color our experiences with our past judgments and interpretations. We can reflect on past experiences mindfully to see what, if anything, we can learn from them, but if we want to live in possibility, we have to set goals based on the present.

POSSIBILITY HAPPENS ONLY IN THE PRESENT

I want to emphasize that possibility happens only in the present. In other words, if you let yourself be controlled by the past-based thinking of the voice in your head, you're not in the present or in the terrain of possibility. When you're not in the present, you're in the world of "could've, would've, should've," and you may be ignoring what's happening in the present altogether.

The way it should be, could have been or would have been is an enemy of possibility. When you're mindful and, therefore, in the present, you let go of past-based judgments and interpretations, whether positive or negative. This allows you to respond with mindful choices about how you're going to achieve what you want based on what is actually happening in the present. This is what makes your goals something that can be, something that is capable of existing.

10

POSSIBILITY—PART II

How we think about or hold life in our minds determines where we want to go and what we want to do. If our minds—our mental machinery—think something is doable, we have a good shot at accomplishing it, and if our machinery thinks it's probably unattainable, we probably won't attain it. The trick is in how we frame our thinking. The magic comes when we mentally hold something as a possibility.

NEGATIVE BELIEFS CREATE NEGATIVE OUTCOMES

When we are filled with negativity, it's impossible to see possibility. We will see only limitations and negativity. Resignation, cynicism, and negativity kill life and all possibility.

As we've discussed, we develop most of our fundamental beliefs about ourselves and the world during our formative years, we carry these beliefs—our Organizing Principles—with us, and they influence our thoughts and actions as adults. Consciously or unconsciously, when we're on automatic pilot, they color our view of everything.

But it doesn't have to be this way. You can change your old and limiting Organizing Principles that were formed in childhood into possibility!

For example, if, when you were a child, the adults around you didn't meet your needs in a consistent, loving way, you might have developed negative, limiting beliefs about yourself and what you can expect of other people. You might have developed the belief that you weren't taken care of because you didn't deserve to be loved and taken care of. This might have resulted in an Organizing Principle like, "I'm not worth much." Or you might have developed an Organizing Principle like, "Nobody will understand or take care of me; I'll always be on my own."

If you believe "I'm not worth being loved and cared for," you are unknowingly sabotaging yourself. You may not express what you want in a relationship because your self-image is that you don't deserve it, or you may express what you want and then still sabotage it because you really don't expect it and have resigned yourself to not getting it.

REPLACING ORGANIZING PRINCIPLES WITH GUIDING PRINCIPLES

Mindfully replacing limiting beliefs with new Guiding Principles opens the door to possibility. Guiding Principles can interrupt your old programming and consciously focus your mind in the present, laying the foundation for the possibility of achieving your goals.

For example, you could replace the Organizing Principle "I'm not worth being loved and cared for" with the Guiding Principle "Other people can like, love, and care for me." You could replace the Organizing Principle "Nobody will understand or take care of me, so I'm going to have to do everything for myself" with the Guiding Principle "Other people can understand and care for me, and I enjoy allowing them to do things for me." You could replace the Organizing Principle "I'll always be on my own" with "I enjoy relationships with other people."

Reflecting on the limitations created by your Organizing Principles will help you phrase your Guiding Principles with words of possibility. Mindfully acting on your new Guiding Principles can influence your thinking and your actions in every area of your life and open the door to possibility!

11

THE LANGUAGE OF POSSIBILITY

The specific language we use when we think and communicate with each other can work for or against us. Here's what I mean.

As we know, we all have a voice in our head and its one purpose is ensuring our survival. It monitors every experience, looking for threats even when there are none, applying what it believes were successful old strategies to present-day situations—often inappropriately. By doing this, it keeps us in the past, making it difficult for us to accomplish our goals.

Everything the voice in our head communicates is expressed in a *language of transition*. This language uses words like *more*, *better*, and *different*. These words focus on becoming something in the future rather than actually being in the present.

The language of transition continues the past into the future by trying to improve situations with old strategies rather than going outside of our old experiences and opening ourselves to new possibilities and transformation. Examples of the language of transition are "Someday I'll have a better job and more money" or "Someday my relationship with my parents will be better."

In contrast, the *language of possibility* allows us to be in the present while opening ourselves up to possibility and transformation. With the language of possibility, we make a simple declaration in the present about the future. Each statement declares the possibility we have to transform whatever problematic situation we're experiencing into the situation we want it to be.

Each statement in the language of possibility starts with "I am the possibility of . . ." In the language of possibility, it's who you want to be that matters—and to become that person, you must give up who and how you have been. For example, "I am the possibility of having a great job with a larger salary" or "I am the possibility of experiencing a good relationship with my parents."

HOW OUR LANGUAGE INFLUENCES OUR RELATIONSHIPS

The way we speak helps us create possibility in our relationships. There are three kinds of speaking:

1. *Descriptive:* This is when you describe what is happening and wait for a response. For example, "Joe, I notice you're asking me the same questions about the deal we're working on." (Then you pause and wait for a response.) Sometimes the statement is followed by a simple inquiry: "Is there some information I'm not providing you?"
2. *Evaluative*: This is when an evaluation of the person's communication is implicit in your response. For example, "Joe, you've been obsessing over this deal." "Obsessing" is an evaluative statement; it is generally considered not good to obsess. Evaluative statements

can also include characterizing the other person: "Joe, you've been whining about this deal." This statement not only evaluates but also says Joe is a whiner.

3. *Interpretive:* This is when you tell the other person what his or her motive or meaning is. Either way, you imply you know what the other person is thinking and that you can access his or her inner world. For example, "Joe, you've been asking me the same questions over and over again, and I think it's because you're insecure about being able to close the deal."

Generally, descriptive statements contain the words *I notice*; evaluative statements begin with the words *you are*, and interpretive statements contain the word *because*.

Evaluative and interpretive statements tend to trigger a defensive response from the other person. Descriptive statements give the person the opportunity to respond in any way that suits him or her. Descriptive statements are compatible with the language of possibility because by not making other people defensive, they create the opportunity for open communication, resolving problems, and transforming relationships.

HOW LANGUAGE CAN HELP US RESOLVE DISAGREEMENTS

We can take risks and face difficult feelings with positive goals when we use the language of possibility.

When a disagreement comes up in a relationship, it opens up the possibility of resolving the situation. You can do this by starting a conversation about it by acknowledging the other person's point of view and saying, "I really see there is truth in your position."

Acknowledgment shows the other person that you are not stuck in your position, that you're big enough and aware enough to truly hear and respect the other person's point of view and to negotiate. Along with the language of possibility and descriptive speaking, acknowledging other people's feelings and points of view is vital to opening the door to possibility and transformation in your relationships.

It's critical to consider the language you use: is it creating a future to live in or one that is destining you to relive the past?

12

ARE YOUR DREAMS OUTSIDE THE LINES?

Walter Mitty, in James Thurber's famous short story "The Secret Life of Walter Mitty," daydreams about heroic deeds while living a very nonheroic life. I call this type of person a *closet outlier.*

My elementary school teacher taught us that it was very important to write "only inside the lines and never outside the lines." It was the same when it came to coloring books: "Color right up to the lines but not outside them." I wonder how Walter Mitty might have lived his life if he'd been encouraged to be expressive no matter what, to create an expanded sense of himself that dared to live large and not be afraid to go outside the lines.

OUTLIERS GO OUTSIDE THE LINES

Oxford Dictionaries defines an outlier as "a person . . . differing from all other members of a particular group or set."[1] In other words, a person who doesn't conform to the characteristics that describe the majority of the group. Metaphorically speaking, an outlier is a person who does things outside the lines. I use the term *inlier* to describe the members of the group who share the majority's characteristics.

Flash forward from childhood instructions and we can see why many of us are inliers, living strictly within the lines, which results in having little flexibility either for living outside the lines ourselves or for people we consider to be living outside the lines.

Many of us are so fixed in our beliefs that we won't (or can't) allow ourselves simple pleasures that we consider outside the lines. When we approach life with this mindset, we limit our behavior in a way that removes many opportunities for spontaneity. We may become wet blankets, prohibiting ourselves from acting in ways that many other people would consider perfectly appropriate. Take, for example, how we dress. Do we stick with a tried-and-true wardrobe, clinging to the same threads and hairstyles for a lifetime, staying away from new and distinctive styles, colors, and fashion statements?

Limiting ourselves to staying within the lines comes at a price. When we censor ourselves by acting automatically in accordance with our interpretations of what our teachers, caretakers, and other "authorities" told us about rules for being right and proper, we do it at the cost of our aliveness and joy.

WHY BEING WALTER MITTY CAN HURT US

Often by their own assessment, the Walter Mittys of the world live a less-than-satisfying life, restricting their aliveness and joy to their daydreams instead of truly experiencing them in their everyday lives. They limit themselves to living inside the lines while denying themselves the self-expression that is at their emotional fingertips.

The question is, why should we put ourselves in a prison that blocks our happiness instead of living fearlessly?

As long as it doesn't hurt anyone else and it's not against the law, let's work at challenging our self-restrictions and give ourselves permission to explore a more expansive, spontaneous, and creative life—and let's encourage and acknowledge others for doing the same!

13

WHY I LOVE PAINTING

I never thought of myself as a writer or artist until I was in my forties. It never occurred to me I had a talent for either. But there was a void in my life—a vacuum, an internal pain. By my midforties I knew that my wife and kids, much as I loved them, couldn't fill the void or heal that pain. It was something I had to do myself. When I got to a low emotional point that was like being in emotional quicksand, I needed something to hold on to so I would not fall deeper.

Back then, my head was filled with judgments and interpretations that said, "This is right" and "This is wrong," about what I could do to heal what I felt to be a lack of connection in my life. Whatever I chose to do, it had to be complementary to my being a family man and a businessman, so I knew that chasing girls and running away with the circus were off the table.

HOW I CAME TO PAINTING

I saw an ad for art classes at Beverly Hills High School. Even though I didn't think I had any artistic talent and the last time I'd done artwork was in third grade, I decided to take the class. Going into the class for the first time, I felt like I was in a retirement community; I was twenty years younger than the next youngest person. (PS—Twenty years later I had the reverse of that experience in acting school, where I was twenty years older than the next oldest and forty years older than the youngest!)

It turned out that I enjoyed the art class. The teacher had a selection of magazines, crayons, colored pencils, and children's water color sets on the table and told us to find an image in a magazine that we liked and draw or paint it. It was sweet sharing with the older people in the class.

I didn't think I was particularly good, but I had fun, and it was better than watching television. The class lasted for three months, and then I had enough confidence to take a class at UCLA Extension, where I found a wonderful teacher who recognized an artistic talent in me long before I saw it myself. That was many years ago, and today I paint several hours every day.

THE REWARDS OF EXPLORING OUR HIDDEN TALENTS

My experience has convinced me that everyone has hidden talents worth exploring.

Taking the chance of going to that art class even though I didn't think I had talent to draw or paint is one of the most valuable things I ever did. I allowed myself to discover that I love painting. The best part of painting for me is being "in the zone." It's the same zone that I experience while swimming or meditating. I believe it connects me to my Higher Self and the collective unconscious that psychoanalyst Carl Jung talks about and that the voice in our head doesn't acknowledge.

The voice in our head has a tendency to want to be the boss, to be center stage, in the limelight, 24/7, with no competition. Painting gives that voice in my head a chew toy just like I give my dogs when I want them to be occupied with something. When I paint, I generally do portraits. My mind is occupied in the same fashion as if I were doing a very intricate crossword puzzle and becomes absorbed in an endless chew-toy fascination with painting. A common joke around my house is that I get kidnapped with and by my painting so that I'm late for dinner.

This kidnapping disempowers the voice in my head by allowing me to exist in a peaceful manner. My self-critic lets go of everything with the exception of an endless need to question if I've gotten the image I'm painting correct. This becomes a wonderful exercise that reminds me that my job is to enjoy the process of painting and to know that the painting I'm doing is my personal creativity from the depths of my self-expression.

Painting gives me the opportunity to let my Higher Self play and to let go of the nuts-and-bolts concerns of the day that my machinery can't let go of on its own. Painting allows unopened windows to open, allowing the fresh breeze of life itself.

14

WHAT I LEARNED IN ACTING SCHOOL

When I was fifty-eight, I saw my friend, a prominent business manager a few years older than me, acting a featured role in a primetime TV show. I was impressed, and it seemed like he was having a great time. I was looking to spice up my life, and seeing him as an actor on TV gave me the idea to follow in his footsteps and try acting, even though, as with painting, I didn't think I had any particular talent for it. I asked my friend how he had come to acting, and then I signed up at the same acting school where he'd taken a two-year course that taught the "Meisner method."

The school was on the second floor of a nondescript office building, but it was filled with attractive young people mingling with each other and excited about acting. I thought, "This is my way of running away and joining the circus," and I enrolled.

DEALING WITH MY SELF-CONSCIOUSNESS

The first night of class arrived, and I felt like a fish out of water. I went to the room I was told to go to and saw twenty uncomfortable-looking folding chairs and one tired old overstuffed chair that looked like the kind you find on street corners in New York, waiting to be recycled by students passing by. Most of the folding chairs were filled by twentysomething Hollywood hopefuls, and although I was fifty-eight, I immediately felt like 158 and thought, "What the hell, I'll go for the comfortable Archie Bunker chair."

A few minutes later, my teacher Elaine Williams came into the class, greeted us, and politely told the 158-year-old to get out of her chair. My acting career had started.

Within ten minutes, she explained legendary acting teacher Sanford Meisner's concept of repetition. She said that the first year of the class would be based on repetition; for me, she might as well have been speaking Martian. I had no clue what she was talking about. She told us to pair up and that two-by-two we would take our places on the stage. One of us, she instructed, would then make a simple observation about the other, and the second person would repeat it back to the first person, who then would repeat it back to the other, and so on.

The moment I heard "pick a partner," I was emotionally right back to being the overweight kid in the sixth grade who was the last person picked to be on the basketball team. Here I was fifty-eight, and fearing no one would choose to partner with me. What twentysomething would want Methuselah as an acting partner?

Much to my surprise, a beautiful young woman chose me to go onto the stage with her. The teacher told her to start, and her observation was "I like your shoes." Now my shoes were older than she was—the classic 1960s loafers with tassels that I'd worn since college. No one under fifty had those shoes; all the other students were wearing the same Doc Martens I took my kids shopping for.

I followed the instructions and repeated, "I like your shoes," back to her, but I did it with the emotional tone of, "Are you making fun of me?" She picked up my implied question and responded back, "I like your shoes," and I got that she was sincere and really liked my shoes.

My internal dialogue said she was being kind to me in the way she would have been to her grandfather. We repeated the phrase to each other at least ten times. I fell asleep that night with a smile on my face, as if I had won a gold medal at the Olympics.

THE UNEXPECTED REWARDS OF STUDYING ACTING

Now, a decade later, I realize that repetition was all about being in the moment. It didn't make any difference what the first person's observation was; the exercise was a way of staying in the now—the present—with your partner, hearing what she or he was really saying as opposed to what you expected to hear.

This lesson had great impact on me in my daily life. It showed me how we often don't listen carefully in our interactions with others, and as a result we hear what we expect to hear and see what we expect to see as opposed to truly listening and seeing. More often than not, this phenomenon makes us misinterpret what is actually being said, which tends to suck the aliveness and joy out of life.

Now I look back on my first day of acting school and see how past based I was in my thinking when I saw myself as an undesirable scene partner—how I mistakenly brought back my self-conscious and unhappy overweight kid self, even though I was no longer that person.

I also now see that I wasn't even that person in sixth grade; I was just another kid who was chubby, not defective, which is how I saw myself at that time. As an adult, I brought that sense of defectiveness right into my acting class. Looking back, I see that I could have said to myself, "Wow, these kids are going to admire someone twice their age having the guts to put himself out there as an actor."

At the end of the two-year period, I had made many friends and was just another member of a family of twenty-five actors.

That two-year class was one of the favorite periods of my life. For me, it was living on the edge and reinventing myself and truly being in the present. Who needs to live in a past that will never be again at the expense of aliveness and joy that is constantly available in the now?

Meisner's definition of acting is to be real in imaginary circumstances. That's what life is—only we think it's real and not imaginary!

LEARNING ABOUT THROUGHLINES

I also learned Meisner's understanding of a *throughline*. Examples of this are John Wayne, Arnold Schwarzenegger, and Sylvester Stallone, who epitomize the strong silent type with "Yup," "Nope," and "I'll be back" throughlines making them the strong, courageous type of man.

I realized that we tend to create our throughlines in life, and even though we may not like them, we may feel that's just the way we are—period. For example, the responsible businessman whose throughline confines him to a life of playing his part like Scrooge in *A Christmas Carol* as opposed to the way of Richard Branson. Branson, founder of Virgin Records and Virgin Atlantic, has a throughline, in addition to being a brilliant businessman, of being a charming and adventurous thrill seeker.

Bottom line: ask for your limitations and they will be granted. I prefer a life with a throughline of endless possibilities.

15

ABUNDANCE VERSUS SCARCITY

My girlfriend and I recently had dinner with two close friends, who asked my girlfriend how she liked living with me and my ninety-six-year-old mother. When she responded, "It's really good," both friends looked at us quizzically, and one of them said, "I'm surprised because Steve's mother has never liked any of his girlfriends. What's your secret?" My girlfriend gave a simple answer, which I summed up as saying that it comes down to her having an abundance of love.

As the conversation continued, we all agreed that my mother has always feared that another woman in my life would lead to my mother being abandoned. Apparently, my mother has a point of view that there isn't enough Steven to love both her and someone else. In other words, my mother comes from the perspective of scarcity.

In contrast, my girlfriend believes there is an infinite amount of love for everyone and everything, including loving and respecting herself and trusting that I have enough love for her and for my mother, my children, and everyone else.

This perspective—that there is an abundance of love—creates the space for happy coexistence with everyone. My girlfriend explained that knowing there is an abundance applies to her acceptance of my mother even when my mother is being critical or hurtful to her, that my girlfriend doesn't need to defend herself or try to change my mother or my mother's way of thinking. She knows that it's just my mother's wiring, and she loves my mother as she is.

THE SAME LOGIC APPLIES IN THE BUSINESS WORLD

The conversation reminded me of a business lunch I had had earlier the same day, discussing the pros and cons of a new and ambitious project.

One of my colleagues—a good, intelligent person and a great businessman—started off with the position that it would be a waste of money to hire attorneys to "paper the project" at this time, and my response was, "I believe we're ready. If we hire the best people and give them the proper road map, the experience will pay for itself one way or the other."

A difference between my colleague's view and mine was that he came from the perspective of scarcity—we can't afford to waste money—while I came from the point of view of abundance. I believed that even if we were to spend the money and then ultimately decide not to pursue the project, it was well worth the gamble, and we wouldn't be affected by the loss since it's only a fraction of 1 percent of our company's worth.

ABUNDANCE AND THE FIRST MOON LANDING

The discussion of abundance versus scarcity made me think about America's space program. Our first astronauts landed on the moon in 1969. In the forty-six years since that first moon landing, there's been an ongoing debate about whether putting men on the moon was worth the expense.

People who come from scarcity say, "What did we get other than a bunch of rocks from the moon, Tang [a powdered orange juice substitute], and Teflon [the metal developed for the heat problem of reentry]?" I, on the other hand, go with the abundance-minded people, who say, "If you add in all of the ancillary technology that was created to get the astronauts back and forth from the moon, it was an incredible return on investment that resulted in technology that's driven the Digital Age."

IT'S UP TO US TO CHOOSE

Like them or not, events both good and bad, and even tragic, happen; the only choice we humans have is how to react to them. Do we react to these events from the perspective of possibility—in which we see an abundant universe with the possibility that we can, despite the obstacles, experience some fulfillment even in extremely challenging situations—or do we react with panic because we believe that the Universe will not support us? Do we see a scarcity of possibility?

The late Dr. Randy Pausch, a professor of computer science at Carnegie Mellon University, became an inspiration to the world when, in his midforties, he was diagnosed with pancreatic cancer and told that he had only a few months to live. A very short time later, on September 18, 2007, he gave "The Last Lecture," about the necessity of maintaining the sense of wonder we have as children and his decision to have fun and enjoy the remainder of his life.

"The Last Lecture" video, seen by millions of people across the Internet, became the basis of a book by the same title, which Dr. Pausch coauthored.[1] Despite knowing that his life would have an early end, Randy Pausch viewed his situation from a perspective of abundance—focusing on the wonders he could experience and enjoy in the time he had instead of looking at his situation from the point of view of scarcity.

I once heard life defined as "a sexually transmitted terminal disease." Looking at life that way, we might as well shoot ourselves at birth. If we look at life as a glorious opportunity to travel the universe for as long as we can, we'll never want to shoot ourselves. The first perspective is coming from scarcity; the second from abundance. The end is the same, but the experience of the voyage is totally different. The choice is ours.

16

THE REWARDS AND CHALLENGES OF TAKING CARE OF MY ELDERLY MOTHER

When my mother was ninety, she still lived on her own in an apartment. She had simple habits. She had a helper who made sure she had lunch and dinner on her table and drove her on errands. The high point of her day was going to Gelson's, an upscale supermarket, where she'd sit for hours over coffee and a sandwich, watching strangers. Most of the people she'd known or spent time with had died long before.

Sunday brunch was the highlight of her week. I'd pick her up, and we'd go to a Beverly Hills deli, where we'd meet my children—her grandchildren—and the waitresses always made her feel special.

It was a good arrangement for all concerned. My mom felt good about being independent, and I carried on with my life, simply calling her a couple of times during the week and doing my dutiful Sunday ritual.

Then things changed. She got a toothache that morphed into an infection, which at ninety could have led to a health disaster if she didn't take the proper care, and she came to stay with me for a few days.

SEEING MY MOTHER THROUGH NEW EYES

I hadn't lived with my mom for over forty years, and her staying with me was an eyeopener—I hadn't realized just how delicate and unsteady on her feet she had become. After a few days she went home, but I felt differently about her. Another couple of weeks went by, and the tooth became a problem again. She moved back to my house, and this time she stayed for good.

I could have found another arrangement such as an assisted-living apartment or having her stay in her own condo with people living in to take care of her, but my personality DNA shouted out, "Family is family! She is my mother!" and "It's my obligation to do the right thing by her!"

Fortunately I have a big house with an extra room and bath and a housekeeper that can help take care of my mother's needs and provide company for her.

MY MOTHER'S PERSONALITY

Taking care of my mother in my house has its rewards and challenges. One reward is seeing firsthand, up close, and very personally, changes that can come with being ninety-six. Witnessing how she has changed in old age has created a comforting model for me, suggesting what may be in store for me in my old age. My mom is super sweet and an inspiration in terms of how aging itself can lessen challenging personality traits.

My mother has always been high drama. She can't separate her feelings from facts. If she feels something is true, nothing can change her mind. In the past, this trait made any perceived insult a call to possible war.

In other words, my mother believed that everything the voice in her head said was actually true, and her fight-or-flight mechanism sprang into action like a rabbit hearing a gunshot. She immediately acted on her beliefs, no matter how far off-base the voice in her head was or what others told her was the truth, and she perceived every situation as a possible disaster. I've always thought of these personality characteristics as her demons.

HOW AGE HAS CHANGED MY MOTHER IN A POSITIVE WAY

Nowadays I see my mother outliving these demons. Though the demons are still there, they no longer have teeth—they have lost their intensity—and she is more even tempered and pleasant company. She reads a few books a week (although she forgets a book as soon as she's read it) and enjoys eating meals with my girlfriend and me, watching a movie with us, and spending time with family and friends who come to the house.

Seeing my mother outlive her demons gives me hope of finding even more joy and peace later in life by outliving mine.

THE CHALLENGES THAT REMAIN

The other side of the coin is seeing that some of her difficult personality traits won't fade! She still embarrasses me by praising me in an over-the-top way that feels to me more like a performance in an opera than normal motherly praise.

But I'm grateful to her for bringing me into the world and for doing the best she could to raise me. This gratitude helps me let go of resentments, both past and present, yet it doesn't prevent me from being fully self-expressed with her if she says something that hurts me. I owe this to myself for my own growth as an authentic person who expresses his feelings with sensitivity and care. But I don't expect what I say to change my mother in a substantial way. I accept that she is who she is.

REVISING THE PAST AND LOOKING INTO THE FUTURE

In addition to the changes I see old age bringing about in my mother's personality, as I mentioned in the chapter "Memories," I also see her rewriting her life story. Until recently, she spoke about herself as having been a Depression-era child living with a passive father who struggled to make enough money to put food on the table and a domineering, emotionally stingy tyrant of a mother who threw my mother's older sister out of the house when my aunt was a teenager. Now my mother tells the story of her childhood as a sentimental, nostalgic movie in which her mother is making cookies and singing her to sleep, while her father, who was a woodworker, finishes one fantastic piece of art after another.

Watching my mother as she rewrites her history and turns a painful childhood into an idyllic one has its inspirational quality. It shows me the possibility of recreating my own history when I'm elderly!

Another fabulous benefit of having my ninety-six-year-old mother living with me is that I can identify with her long life instead of the short life of my dad, who died at thirty-eight.

I can disavow my dad's genetics and hope that my longevity genes came from Mom's side.

Most of all, taking care of my mother in her old age is helping me to grow into a more understanding and compassionate person.

Thanks, Mom!

Pause Your Machinery

The previous eight chapters have covered a lot of ground; now it's time to do a few exercises. Be sure to write out your thoughts. The effort and concentration it takes will make the exercises more helpful.

- Reflect mindfully on areas in your life in which you feel that you're not achieving your goals, personal or professional. Ask yourself whether you are looking at your goals through the filter of your past-based programming. If so, describe how your past experiences are influencing your expectations about achieving these goals. Describe whether they are having a negative influence on your vision about what you can achieve.
- Now mindfully change your perspective and write a statement of your goals using the language of possibility. Describe what this new and different outlook does in terms of opening the door to potential fulfillment.
- Remember my description of the rich rewards I had taking art and acting classes and the joy I feel every day as I oil paint. Are there activities you would like to do—talents you would like to explore—which, although they wouldn't hurt anybody, you have considered outside the lines? If so, list them and describe the judgments that have been holding you back from pursuing them. Look mindfully at these judgments and the limitations you impose on yourself by believing them, let go of the belief that you need to stay inside the lines, and describe the avenues you want to pursue in the language of possi-

bility. Now describe what you will do to start exploring these activities and talents.

- Reflect on whether you come from a perspective of abundance or a perspective of scarcity. If you don't know immediately which perspective you come from, ask yourself: Do I tend to feel that there is enough love to go around or that I have to compete for love, even in my closest relationships? Do I feel that there is an abundance of good feelings? Do I feel that there is an abundance of opportunity?

  If you find that you are coming from scarcity, mindfully ask yourself if you're willing to change your point of view. If so, describe the steps you're going to take to change your perspective and also describe how this change will affect the way you will pursue your goals and the emotional tone of your daily life.
- If there is an elderly relative in your life whom you take care of or whom you see on a regular basis, describe this person and how you feel about him or her. Mindfully reflect on and describe what that person is going through as he or she ages. Undoubtedly there are challenges in your relationship with the person. Describe the challenges, and reflect on and write about his or her wiring and your own wiring. Does looking at that person from the perspective of wiring add to your compassion? Does looking at your relationship from the perspective of the differences between your wiring and his or hers allow you to see more clearly the factors that create the challenges? Does this change your attitude toward the

person and the relationship in any way? If so, describe how it changes it.

Part III

IMPROVING YOUR COMMUNICATION WITH OTHERS

17

COMMUNICATING FROM SEPARATE VIRTUAL REALITIES

Why, even in our closest relationships, do we agree on some things and disagree on others? It's because no matter how close we are to each other, we each still live in our own separate and unique *virtual reality*, which is shaped by our individual perceptions and interpretations of the world around us.

This unique virtual reality is determined by the specific way our brain is wired. As I've mentioned, our wiring depends on nature and nurture. Nature includes biological characteristics we are born with, some of which we have in common with most other people and some that vary from individual to individual. Nurture—our environment—includes our particular experiences from infancy on, especially our experiences with our parents or other caretakers, that form our default programming that helps to shape our wiring or neural circuitry.

HOW NATURE AND NURTURE INFLUENCE OUR VIRTUAL REALITY

On the nature side, some of the traits we are born with that we share with other people include crying when we're hungry and laughing when we're tickled. Also part of nature are some specific personal traits that result from the genes we inherit. But our individual programming, which is embodied in our wiring, develops uniquely from nurture; it begins as a blank slate that we fill in with the rest of our characteristics and abilities as we grow and develop.

This includes the attitudes we form. For example, we start out with a blank-slate attitude toward dogs and cats and, depending on our experiences, we may eventually turn out to be a cat person, a dog person, a dog and cat person, or a person who just doesn't like pets. In the same way, depending on the experiences we have and the attitudes we develop, we may find some things funny and other things not funny, while others will have the opposite response.

HOW WE GET TAKEN BY SURPRISE

Sometimes we feel we have so much in common with another person that we consider that person our soul mate, and we assume our soul mate's virtual reality is identical to ours. But each virtual reality is so vast and individualized that one person's can't possibly be exactly the same as another's.

Consider each virtual reality as being as unique as a fingerprint. From a distance, one person's fingerprint may look the same as the fingerprint of another person, but viewed through a magnifying glass, differences become clear. It's the same with our virtual realities.

But unlike fingerprints, which we and others can see, virtual realities are an inner experience. No one can completely experience another's virtual reality. The only way we can learn about other people's virtual realities is through our observations of their external behavior—that is, what they say and do—and they can only learn about ours the same way.

Adding to the complexity is that we are all affected by multiple levels of emotions, which contain conflicting feelings that we intentionally or unconsciously hide from other people and sometimes even unconsciously hide from ourselves in our dark side (see chapter 5).

Another challenging element is that our virtual reality is always a work in progress; it's never a fully developed finished product. Every day we experience new things, and with these new experiences our virtual reality evolves; new aspects emerge and develop as we encounter new forks in the road of life.

WHEN WE CAN RESOLVE DIFFERENCES AND WHEN WE CAN'T

As we've discussed, every breakdown is caused by one of three situations:

1. Unfulfilled expectations
2. Thwarted intentions
3. Incomplete communications

When we experience one of these—when we expect something and don't get it, intend to achieve something and don't, or want to understand another person or have that person understand us and this doesn't occur to our satisfaction—we often blame the other person for our disappointment or anger. When people can't resolve a breakdown harmoniously, often it's because one or both people want to dominate the other person—to win—declaring themselves right and making the other person wrong. That's the nature of conflicts.

That's why it's vital to recognize that *a breakdown is simply a clash of two virtual realities seeing the same situation with different interpretations.* To resolve a breakdown harmoniously, both people need to respect each other's perspective and experience—the other's virtual reality—as a starting point for finding common ground.

18

THE I-MESSAGE VERSUS THE YOU-MESSAGE

Psychologists often advise that when telling someone how you feel, it's important to use an I-message rather than a you-message. This is especially important if you're expressing something the other person would interpret as negative. For example, if you feel upset by something a friend has said, instead of saying, "You're upsetting me," you would say, "I felt upset when I heard that."

THE DIFFERENCE BETWEEN I-MESSAGES AND YOU-MESSAGES

On the most basic level, when you express your feelings with a you-message, you are likely to make other people defensive because a you-message tells them that they are responsible for your feelings: "*You made* me upset." In contrast, expressing your feelings with an I-message simply describes the way you feel—"*I felt* upset"—but it doesn't say that someone else is responsible for your feelings.

In reality, other people are not responsible for your feelings; nobody makes you feel as you do. Your feelings are part of your inner world, and how you react emotionally to the outer world—your responses to other people and to the circumstances you encounter—depends on how your inner world is interpreting the situation.

Your inner world is your machinery and your programming (the way you think and act when you're on automatic pilot, which is based on your mind's interpretations of earlier experiences). How you respond emotionally to a situation depends on whether you allow your machinery and programming to run on automatic pilot, which keeps you in the past, or whether you interrupt your machinery so that you are in the present moment instead of being controlled by your past programming. If you're on automatic pilot, the emotions you feel in response to what another person says or does in the present are actually reactions not to the current situation but to a past situation that your machinery likens to the current situation.

HOW I-MESSAGES COMMUNICATE WHAT WE ARE FEELING

Let's say, for example, you had a highly critical parent who repeatedly called you stupid as a child, and now you're an adult in a relationship with someone who points out to you that you've made a mistake. If you're on automatic pilot, the mere fact that the other person said you made a mistake will make you feel awful. It will bring back the humiliation you felt when your parent called you stupid. But you won't be aware of why you're feeling this way: it's not because you're responding to the actual situation in the present but because your machinery has been triggered to react with awful feelings from your childhood experience.

In a situation like this, it's clear that an I-message—"I felt upset when you said I made a mistake"—communicates the truth of exactly what happened. You felt upset when the other person said you made a mistake. He or she did not make you feel upset. You felt upset because your machinery and the past experiences that shaped your programming triggered you to feel the upset from your childhood experience all over again.

Again, this generally happens when you allow your machinery to run on automatic pilot instead of manually interrupting your machinery and being in the present. By manually interrupting, I mean focusing your mind on the present and shifting your mental gears so that you're no longer on automatic pilot.

I-MESSAGES HELP US TO BE MINDFUL

Expressing yourself with an I-message about your feelings will support you in manually interrupting your machinery. It can remind you to start reflecting on why you are feeling upset, to notice that you have been letting your machinery run on automatic pilot, and to start mindfully reflecting on what is happening.

Once you interrupt your machinery and start being mindful—paying attention in the present with an open, rather than a judgmental, mind—ask yourself, Am I reacting emotionally to what is going on right now or to something that happened a long time ago and that my machinery is interpreting the current situation to be like?

Once you start being mindful, ask yourself, Did I hear the comment about my making a mistake as judgmental because it was actually said judgmentally or because of the way that I interpreted it?

One of my cardinal rules is that *when your machinery is running you on automatic pilot, you hear what you expect to hear and see what you expect to see* based on your past programming.

When you're mindful and are in the present, you can tell the difference between your past-based expectations of what you will hear and see and what is actually taking place. When this happens, even if you've started to react based on your programming, you will begin to hear and see the current circumstance clearly instead of being mindless and unconsciously mistaking it for a repetition of the past.

I often find myself in this situation when someone tells me that I've made a mistake. If I'm on automatic pilot, then no matter how the other person tells me about the mistake, I hear it as, "You are wrong! You are bad!" and I feel shamed and blamed. This is because when I'm on automatic pilot, my own inner critic—which is contained in my programming—is running me, and it amplifies whatever it interprets as criticism into a storm of criticism. So on automatic pilot, I don't hear what the other person is really saying; I just start reacting and defending myself or attacking the other person with the defensive strategies contained in my programming to get rid of the awful feeling of shame and blame.

I've learned that the intensity of my reaction is a clue that I'm on automatic pilot. When I recognize this clue, I interrupt my machinery and start to become mindful.

Being mindful changes everything. Instead of feeling upset and ashamed—the feelings you had in the situation with your critical parent—you may feel appreciative to have had the mistake pointed out because it gives you a chance to correct it. Instead of "I feel upset," the I-message would then become "I'm grateful you told me about it."

The I-message accurately reports how you feel without blaming the other person for your feelings. It also gives you the opportunity to share more of yourself to give the other person insight into who you are and how the two of you can communicate better and create a more fulfilling relationship with each other.

19

SILENCE: WHEN IS IT GOOD AND WHEN IS IT UNPRODUCTIVE?

I was in an important meeting with a business associate recently. Our relationship had been strained, so we used a psychologist to facilitate as we tried to resolve our disagreement, and she was in the meeting, too. The day after the meeting, the facilitator e-mailed us her summation of the meeting. I was taken aback to find that her summary stated I'd agreed to a point I had not agreed to.

I called her, wanting to understand how and why her summation didn't correspond with mine. To my surprise, she explained that my associate made a proposal and then went on to discuss his point of view for quite some time while I listened and approved. Actually, I did not approve of my colleague's proposal; I disagreed with it but was willing to listen and mull it over. She mistakenly interpreted my silence as approval.

Even though I thought it was inappropriate for the facilitator to interpret my silence as agreement, I understood how my silence gave her the opportunity to misinterpret my point of view. This made me think about silence as a communication tool—when it helps and when it's a hindrance.

WHEN I GO SILENT

I've come to understand that I have a tendency to shut down in confrontational situations that provoke anxiety in me. I may stay quiet out of fear my responses will exacerbate the situation or I will appear defensive or aggressive, so it's safer to remain silent.

There are other situations in which I am silent as well. For example, sometimes I'm silent when someone starts a discussion in which it sounds like he or she is asking for advice but I sense that person really just wants to vent and receive my empathetic response. Prior to becoming sensitive to this, I generally used to go into problem-solving mode; now I realize that compassionately making space with silence is often the best thing for a friend to do.

SILENCE AND COMPLEXES

I discussed the concept of complexes in chapter 3. Jung defined a complex as a complete minipattern of autonomous behaviors that lives in the shadowy recesses of the unconscious and can kidnap your reactions without your being aware of it.[1] Jung believed that complexes result from our childhood emotional traumas.

When Jung says that a complex is *autonomous*, he means that it operates on its own; we're not aware that we have the complex, how it affects us, or when we are in it, and yet it has the power to possess us.

The most problematic part of being in a complex is that we lose touch with everything that is going on in the present; nothing exists for someone in a complex outside of his or her immediate, intense perceptions and emotions. These are the times people say things to a partner like, "You never loved me"—forgetting all the love their partner has shown them and the good things their partner does for them. While in the complex, it's as if those good things never happened.

When I'm with someone who is that worked up, I realize that nothing I say or do will get through to him or her—so silence becomes a helpful tool. I know that we can talk later, when the person is no longer in the complex.

SILENCE AND DIGITAL TECHNOLOGY

These days, upsetting e-mails or text messages can get me emotionally activated—kidnapped by a complex. These digital communications have the power to trigger in me the same upsets as voice-to-voice or face-to-face communications can, and I've learned that at times like these, silence can be helpful. I've trained myself to wait at least two hours before responding to these digital communications so I can regain my emotional equilibrium, reflect on the message with objectivity, and respond mindfully instead of defensively. The payoff of doing this is a better chance to negotiate differences of opinion and more harmony in my relationships.

SELF-EXPRESSION IS THE KEY

I believe that full self-expression—communicating how we think and feel—is the key to good relationships. Silence can be an appropriate part of how we interact with others who simply want to be listened to. But as I've learned, we have to be mindful about how we use silence so that we won't be misinterpreted.

20

WHEN YOU HAVE TROUBLE SAYING NO

I have little trouble saying yes or no in my business life. The criteria for saying yes or no are always very clear to me: Will the action be good or bad for the business? Is it something that is in keeping with my integrity or out of alignment with my integrity?

Not only are these criteria very clear to me, I also immediately know the answer. I don't even need to think about it. As soon as the question is asked, I know right away when I need to say no. And because it's so clear to me, no matter how much I like the person who's brought me the issue I have to decide on, if I feel that no is the appropriate answer, I have no trouble saying no. And if he or she asks me to explain why I'm saying no, I can do it easily.

It's a completely different story in my personal life. Because of my fear of abandonment, it's always been almost impossible for me to say no—at least to say no and stick with it—to my family members and closest friends. Even if I was clear that a no was the appropriate decision—for example, that something was too expensive or an elaborate birthday party was too over-the-top—I would become filled with anxiety, and the fact that saying no was the right decision would be less important than doing what I felt was necessary to keep the other person happy.

Of course, this makes no sense in the long run because a wrong decision always catches up to us. If we buy a child or a teenager something that's more expensive than is appropriate for a person of that age, he or she is going to continue expecting things that are inappropriate. But knowing that saying no was the responsible decision in situations with family and close friends didn't make it easier for me.

BECOMING CLEAR ABOUT MY PROGRAMMING

What made me act so irrationally that I would say yes when I knew that no was appropriate? What made me act in a way that was against my true feelings and the interest of the other person whom I cared for so much? Why was saying no so easy for me to do at work and so hard for me to do at home? The reason comes down to my programming.

As a child, I had two powerful experiences that profoundly shaped my programming and that much later in life could still put me into an emotional blur when I was placed in a situation of having to say yes or no to someone very close to me. The first experience was the traumatic loss of my father when I was eleven, and the second was that I saw my mother cut off members of her family with whom she had conflicts; if someone disagreed with her, suddenly that person was gone from my life!

These experiences made my child's mind forever fearful that anyone I love very much could just vanish, especially if there was a conflict. Because my mother cut off people with whom she had conflicts, I developed a conscious belief that the way to have people you love stay in your life was to agree to give them everything they wanted; if you didn't disagree with them, they wouldn't abandon you.

After a while, by continually avoiding disagreements from childhood on, I didn't even know what I wanted for myself anymore, except that I didn't want people to cut me off as my mother had done to her family, to abandon me as my father had done by dying.

Sometimes I avoided confrontations by not really defining my position. In my heart, I knew my decision was no, but fearing a conflict, I would say something vague like, "I'll think about it," or I wouldn't address it at all (staying silent, as I write about in chapter 21). Sometimes I hoped the issue would go away before I had to give an answer. This really doesn't work!

LEARNING TO SAY NO

If you have a problem saying no, the first step to becoming better at saying no when it's appropriate is to learn to recognize why it's a problem for you. What is activating your machinery? What are the beliefs and assumptions in your programming? What is causing you to be fearful about saying no?

I took this first step when, through therapy, I realized that saying no was a problem for me, that every time I felt I should say no to a person I love I was unconsciously afraid that saying no would mean I'd be abandoned. With this recognition, I realized the anxiety I felt in such situations was caused by an *inauthentic fear*—a fear that feels as if it's related to survival but is actually not about survival. This is just left over as a result of a dysfunctional pattern developed in childhood.

This helped me take the second step, which is the recognition that we have the power to act despite our fears and that if we give in to inauthentic fears and say yes when we want to say no, we are not honoring our integrity. Not only does this feel bad because we sense that we're doing something that's not truthful to who we are, it's often bad for the other person, too, and it's bad for our relationship with that person.

Buying love—whether literally with money or by doing something that you don't want to do—isn't good if you want a relationship to thrive. A thriving relationship needs both people to communicate and act with integrity, and a conflict can be an opportunity for growth in a thriving relationship.

If you have a problem saying no, the solution lies in the following:

- Making the commitment to become aware of how your machinery and its programming work with regard to this issue.
- Backing up this commitment with your will to transform yourself so you remain aware and interrupt your machinery to make a conscious choice. (See chapter 7.)
- Recognizing when and why your machinery becomes activated when you have trouble saying no and becoming aware of the negative consequences of remaining on automatic pilot and being run by your past-based programming. This motivates you to interrupt your machinery and make the mindful choice to say no when you need to—and to stick to it.

Even if saying no makes you anxious, remember that thriving relationships can withstand and grow from disagreements. If you say yes when your integrity tells you that you need to say no, you are undermining not only yourself but also the very relationship that you value.

Pause Your Machinery

Recognizing different points of view and communicating effectively about them may take some practice. Here are some exercises to help you reflect on your experiences and develop these important skills.

- If there is someone in your life whom you have difficulty resolving arguments with, reflect mindfully on a recent situation where the two of you disagreed. Describe how the other person viewed it and how you viewed it. Mindfully reflect on the differences between your points of view, and describe the differences between your virtual reality in regard to that situation and the other person's. Now reflect on whether each of you respected the other's perceptions. Did you attempt to resolve your disagreement by starting from respect for each other's perceptions? Do you think that seeing such disagreements from the point of view of conflicting virtual realities will help you discuss and resolve disagreements in the future? If so, describe the steps you'll take to communicate respectfully and work to resolve disagreements when disagreements come up.
- Reflect mindfully on recent situations in which you've felt hurt by or angry at another person. In these situations, did you use an I-message or a you-message ("I felt hurt when you said . . ." versus "You hurt me by saying . . ." or "I felt angry when you said . . ." versus "You made me angry when you said . . .")?

  If you used a "you message," reflect mindfully on whether this made the other person defensive and harder for him or her to acknowledge your feelings and understand why you felt hurt or angry. If you think that you would benefit from your using I-messages instead of you-messages, describe the steps you will take to make this change.

- Reflect mindfully on whether you use silence productively or in ways that lead to misunderstandings. If you see that you do use it in dysfunctional ways, describe a recent incident in which your silence led to a misunderstanding. Now describe what you will do in the future to express yourself clearly and avoid misunderstandings.
- Reflect mindfully on whether you have trouble saying no. If you do, describe two or three recent situations in which you would have liked to say no but didn't. Then describe the reason you didn't say no. Reflect on what these situations have in common. Were you afraid of a particular reaction if you said no? Reflecting on your past, can you see interactions in your childhood or later that led to a fear of saying no becoming part of your default programming? If you would like to change and become fully self-expressed, write a new Guiding Principle that will empower you to say no when you want to.

Part IV

WHAT MAKES RELATIONSHIPS WORK (AND NOT WORK)

21

I THOUGHT SHE WAS MYSTERIOUS BUT ACTUALLY SHE WAS JUST DEPRESSED

We are all reaction machines. Something happens and we react. In fact, we can't not react; our only choice is *how* we react. Each of us reacts in our unique way, based on our individual interpretation of what just happened—and we all may see it differently. As I discussed in chapter 17, no matter how close we feel to someone, that person may react to the same situation differently from the way we react to it because we all live in our own virtual reality, even though most of us mistakenly assume that the other person will see what just happened exactly the way we do.

This is why it's important to remember that everyone has his or her own one-of-a-kind programming or virtual reality, which includes its unique belief systems.

But it's easy to forget this. When we're on automatic pilot—not mindfully aware about what we're experiencing in the present moment—our default programming is running us and influencing our perceptions. As we know, this programming, which is based on our past experiences, influences our reactions to current situations by evaluating them in the context of how we felt about previous situations it judges to be similar. It affects the way we see, experience, and—if we let it—react to everything and everyone we encounter.

The problem is that when we're on automatic pilot and our default programming triggers us to misinterpret something in the present, no matter how wrong our perception may be, we view our interpretation as the way it is; we believe that our feeling is a fact instead of simply our interpretation.

For example, I was in a romantic relationship with a woman who was often quiet. At first I thought she was mysterious, and that was a real turnon. She seemed wise, and her silence made her seem even wiser. I thought that she never needed to say or do anything because she was waiting for us "smaller brains" to work our way to her conclusions.

It took me more than a year to gradually recognize and accept that her mysterious ways were actually masking a lack of self-esteem and the depression that accompanied it. I also came to recognize that my misperception was an outgrowth of my own default programming; I had built her up in my mind because I wanted to see her as possessing something I was lacking.

STRONG AND SILENT OR JUST INSECURE?

A woman friend of mine met a man she experienced as being sure of himself, quick to take control, and a born leader—and she married him. Eventually she realized that her husband's take-charge actions were a result of a deep-seated insecurity that made him too fearful to trust others.

Both my friend and I had partners who rarely shared their deepest feelings or apologized. Each of us initially thought our partners were so "together" (in the security department) that they didn't need to share or apologize. Like me, my friend gradually realized that her first impression of her husband was based on her own lack of self-worth. Eventually we both broke up with our partners.

WHAT MAKES A GOOD RELATIONSHIP?

For me, the important point to recognize is that although our relationships start off with our first impressions, ultimately they continue or break up based on our attunement to each other. We may start out with a misperception of another person we become romantically involved with, but that doesn't mean the relationship is doomed. The vital quality in a relationship is communication. If both people are interested in growing together, they can find common ground and learn to become attuned to each other and to fulfill each other's needs. What broke up the relationships I described was the lack of attunement; we and our partners didn't find a common ground and we stopped sharing our thoughts and feelings, so we simply couldn't be attuned.

I've learned that where you start out in a relationship is never as important as where you go from there!

22

JUDGING OTHERS

In my book *My Mind Is Not Always My Friend: A Guide for How to Not Get in Your Own Way,*[1] I say that when we stop judging, love is everywhere. By judging, I mean negatively evaluating other people's actions or words and expressing our evaluation to them in some way.

When we judge others, we are literally passing judgment on them. This puts a barrier between them and us, and it discourages trust, communication, intimacy, and loving feelings. That's why it's important to gain insight into our habit of judging others and to learn to be less judgmental.

As we know, the voice in our head, which comes from our machinery and relays judgments to us, has one job: to keep us safe so we'll survive. Our mind is constantly evaluating everything, looking for anything it senses as a potential danger, and our machinery reacts instantly to everything that is scanned. The reaction can be anything from a positive judgment that something is safe to a negative judgment that it's a threat. If it's a threat, our reaction may be some form of fight or flight. Fight or flight can mean physically running away, or it can mean shutting down emotionally or verbally attacking the person whom the machinery interprets to be a threat (or even physically defending ourselves in the case of a physical threat).

The biggest problem is that when we're on automatic pilot, our machinery can trigger us to perceive our judgment as if it's a fact as opposed to being just a feeling.

Before I recognized this, my inner world went to war over my judgments because I didn't know the difference between a feeling and a fact. For me, everything was black and white, right or wrong, yes or no, my way or the highway, and every judgment had intense emotion behind it. If I felt that someone threatened me—which might mean I interpreted the person as putting me down or criticizing me—I'd attack the person to defend myself.

WHAT HAPPENS WHEN WE FEEL THREATENED

In situations in which we feel threatened, our machinery often reacts instantly and preemptively, even though frequently there is no real problem, just a misinterpretation on the machinery's part. For example, the machinery may interpret someone's disagreeing with us as a danger, and we judge the other person as wrong and instantly defend ourselves. A disagreement isn't, in fact, a threat, and neither is a criticism.

If you can put your judgment aside and really hear and open your mind to what the other person is saying, a disagreement or even a criticism can lead to your learning something new about yourself or gaining a new perspective on the situation that you and the other person are involved in. And this may lead to a resolution that will be good for you both.

THE NEGATIVE EFFECT OF JUDGING OTHERS

I have a friend whose mother taught her that "there's a correct way and an incorrect way to do everything." After being raised by a mother who instructed her on what constitutes correct manners, how to dress correctly, what kind of furniture is in good taste, and the concept that there is a correct way to do everything in life, my friend has trouble not passing judgment on people around her whom she sees doing things that are incorrect—in other words, doing things their own way instead of her way, the way her mother taught her was correct.

This has led my friend to the habit of being judgmental with her husband and adult children, which makes them annoyed with her. Once she recognized that her judgments come from her programming, it became easier for her to be mindful that just because she thinks that it's incorrect when, for example, her husband cooks dinner a certain way or wears a certain shirt with a certain pair of pants, doesn't mean that it's actually incorrect. She's had to not make judgmental remarks to him or, in similar situations, her children, who are now adults.

The challenge, she readily admits, is that when she sees something she perceives as incorrect, she feels it so strongly that she thinks it's a fact. Again, the trouble is that feelings aren't facts, even though we think they are.

This judging process is *solid state*—that is, the mind generally doesn't weigh the issue but instead, when we're on automatic pilot, reacts in a nanosecond and not in proportion to the situation.

WHAT TO DO WHEN JUDGMENTS COME UP

Here is a rule of thumb: silent judgments can exist without causing conflict between us and others, but when we act on our judgments with words, deeds, or even body language, they become voiced judgments, which can cut the other person—sometimes like a butter knife, sometimes like a meat cleaver.

It's important to keep judgments to ourselves until we've had time to process them and make a conscious choice about how accurate our perception is and how we want to respond to the other person. When I do this, often I realize that my judgment is off base, and there's no need for me to say anything.

A companion to "feelings are not facts" is another rule I find helpful: you can't argue with another person's perceptions. One of my Guiding Principles that arises from this rule is that conflicting feelings can coexist peacefully until you attach an action to them. When two people see the same thing differently, as long as actions are not attached to these opposing feelings, a situation might be uncomfortable, but it will be bearable.

Problems arise when the feelings burst into behavior in which the two people's machineries go to war. A prime example of this situation is when two people are angry at each other and one of them attaches an action to his feelings by punching the other in the jaw. As long as we don't attach actions to our opposing-viewpoint feelings, we hold out the potential for creating the opportunity to talk about our feelings accurately and without judgment while remembering that feelings are feelings, not facts.

The most effective way to stop our judging process is to stay in the present—to focus consciously on the here and now and make mindful choices rather than acting on automatic pilot. When we are mindful, we know the harm that being judgmental of others—and of ourselves—can do, and we let go of our judgments and allow them to dissolve instead of holding on to them.

23

ARE YOU A FROG IN HOT WATER?

When I was a kid, one of my teachers said that if a frog was placed in a pan of lukewarm water that was put on the stove with the flame on simmer, the frog would acclimate as the temperature rose, stay in the pan, and eventually perish when the water got too hot. The story stuck with me, though I later learned that it wasn't true; in reality, when the water heats up too much, the frog will jump out of the pan.

People, on the other hand, often stay in bad relationships that get progressively worse, acclimatizing to their increasing suffering. Metaphorically speaking, they are analogous to the frogs in hot water in my teacher's apocryphal story, experiencing more and more emotional pain as the water (or tone of the relationship) gets hotter and hotter (or worse and worse) and yet staying there, sometimes for their entire lives.

A few years ago, after I left a three-decade relationship, I wanted to understand why I stayed in a situation that was so uncomfortable for its last ten years. My thinking about my own frog-in-hot-water relationship has brought me greater clarity about it, especially about my own role in creating it and remaining in it. Here's what I discovered.

VICTIMS AND TWEAKERS

When we're in a frog-in-hot-water type of relationship, often we see ourselves as victims, being "unfaired against" by family, friends, or business colleagues. In my case, I kept trying to fix the situation, and when my strategy didn't work, I would tweak it, feeling sure it would work eventually if I got it exactly correct. That old adage "Insanity is doing the same thing over and over and expecting a different result" applied to me. I kept being the frog in hot water, believing that my partner would eventually "see the light" because we loved each other and that our problems would disappear.

HOW OUR OWN MYTHS HURT US

Reflecting on my ten years as a frog in hot water, I came to understand that often we remain in hot water because of a myth we believe is true. The myth I believed was that I was emotionally defective and my partner was emotionally sound. Subscribing to this myth, I thought if I could show her my heart was in the right place, she would understand and the hot water would instantly cool. I saw myself as a victim of my own emotional defectiveness and believed it was the reason I couldn't access her love. Now I understand that there are always myths that keep us like frogs in hot water. As long as I believed my myth, I felt helpless.

I now see that my partner also had a myth. Hers was that she deserved a Prince Charming who would always do the right thing according to her script of what the right thing was, and that if he didn't, he was in the wrong. By the time we entered what eventually became the last ten years of our relationship, she had come to the conclusion that I didn't match her idea of doing the right thing.

We can make ourselves the hero or the victim in any story, regardless of how our partner experiences the situation. We turn our experiences into stories we believe are true, and when we're on automatic pilot we believe that eventually everyone else, particularly our partners, will see things as we do and arrive at the same conclusions. We don't realize that our story is just our story—our interpretation of events based on our individual perceptions—and that it won't necessarily match our partner's perceptions.

REINTERPRETING OUR EXPERIENCE

Being a frog in hot water is a direct consequence of forgetting that our story is really our feeling and instead calling it a fact or the truth. We forget that our story is not cast in stone; we are always free to reinterpret what we are experiencing and tell ourselves another story about it. When we do this, we're no longer a frog in hot water; we no longer see ourselves as powerless victims.

THE THREE DOORS

Remember, there are always three possible ways to respond to any situation, including a frog-in-hot-water situation. I think of these possibilities as Door 1, Door 2, and Door 3. Let's look at these solutions in detail.

Door 1 is to accept the situation fully, warts and all. This means acknowledging the situation exactly as it is and saying, "I'm okay with it. I'm letting go of my judgments and resentments." It means that we stop resisting the situation and instead embrace it. When we embrace the situation instead of judging, resisting, and resenting it, the water ceases to be hot—the pain disappears.

Door 2 is to change the situation. This means working out a meaningful solution by making mindful choices that will transform the situation in a way that meets our needs and the other's needs. Of course, for Door 2 to work, both people have to commit to moving beyond past pain and into a future of possibility for a new experience of the relationship. Both people need to let go of their old resentments and judgments.

Door 3 is to remove ourselves entirely from the situation—the frog has to acknowledge that the water is too hot and it's in danger of being killed, and then it must jump out of the pan.

GAINING INSIGHT INTO YOUR OWN BEHAVIOR

The vital thing to remember is that choosing Door 3 to exit a particular frog-in-hot-water situation only alleviates the pain from that particular situation. It takes recognizing and acknowledging your participation in the painful situation and constant mindfulness not to repeat that pattern of behavior that helped to create it.

Remember, the way to free ourselves from a frog-in-hot-water situation is to mindfully observe our own patterns of behavior and then change that behavior. Whatever the situation, we will always find ourselves with the choice of Doors 1, 2, or 3.

24

SHEDDING EXPIRED RELATIONSHIPS

In a recent therapy session, I was working through painful problems in a close friendship. The breakdown in the relationship has to do with money. I've found that an abundance of money can be both a blessing and a curse because we can confuse love with money. In other words, people can perceive that the more money someone gives them, the more that person loves them, and if that person doesn't give them what they perceive to be enough, that person doesn't love them.

In the past I've unintentionally supported this misperception in some people close to me because, as I wrote in chapter 20, "When You Have Trouble Saying No," it's been very hard for me to say no to those I love, and when I did, I've often felt guilty. So, to avoid conflict and keep the relationship in place, frequently I've thrown money at a problem when I've known I should have said no.

I've grown over the years, and as a result I am no longer willing to throw money at a significant other, friend, or family member out of my fear that, if I don't, the other person won't love me. I've come to understand that in some relationships I was enabling destructive behavior in the same way giving money to a drug addict enables drug addiction. I've also come to understand that by throwing money at a relationship, I've shortchanged myself, all because of my own fear of abandonment.

WHEN SAYING NO CAUSES A BREAK IN A RELATIONSHIP

When I've lost a relationship because I said no, I notice that I'm fine with the situation, and yet I can find myself still experiencing something like *phantom pain* (the pain that an amputee can feel in the place of an amputated limb), which I believe is part of the grieving process over the loss of the relationship.

I've come to understand that as we grow, we shed the expired relationships from our lives like we shed old skin or the way a bird sheds loose feathers or a tree sheds dried leaves; in other words, if we are wise, we realize we have the opportunity to shed what no longer serves us. Some of those expired relationships are relationships that have become toxic to us.

I experience both comfort and pain in this understanding. I understand it is necessary to recognize and shed relationships that no longer serve us, and yet the voice in my head doesn't want to accept that I would let someone I've been so close to fade away from my daily life. The voice keeps telling me I love that person and it's wrong to let the relationship go into suspended animation or die. Even with relationships that have become toxic, the voice in my head continues to tell me that somehow our relationship will magically repair and all I have to do is wait with patience.

At the same time, I know that nothing works without integrity, and a friendship or any other personal relationship based on payment—whether material or emotional—isn't really a healthy relationship.

CHOOSING TO BE HEALTHY

Today, my life is the best it's ever been. I'm stronger internally and clearer than ever before, which is why I now have the emotional strength to be true to myself and let the chips fall where they may—yet it's still hard.

I also know that every day holds the possibility of creating a new friendship with the same person I previously shed, a relationship that will be healthier than the old one if we can both grow and change. There always has to be a breakdown before there can be a breakthrough.

25

BEING SINGLE

I was twenty-two when I first got married. This was before the birth-control pill, legalized abortion, and the sexual freedom born in the hippie era. The word *relationship* wasn't in my universe. The idea of hooking up with a woman without getting married meant, in my mind, that she would instantly become pregnant and then there would be a shotgun marriage or an illegal abortion, which was extremely dangerous. I still believed the 1950s notion I'd grown up with that having sex with a girl outside of marriage was taking advantage of her.

Back then I was filled with bodily shame from being an overweight adolescent, and, as I mentioned in chapter 23, I saw myself as somewhat defective in the feeling department. These self-perceptions contributed to a belief system in which I pictured myself at the end of a long line of more desirable guys vying for the attention of the girls I thought were cool.

After nine years of marriage to my high school sweetheart, we divorced. It was the era of the sexual revolution, the hippie movement, and protests against the war in Vietnam. I was thirty-one, successful, slim, running six miles a day, and in therapy. But my inner-world sense of self hadn't changed very much, and I believed it was due to sexual repression, resulting from having had only one lover, my former wife. I thought that the fantasy new lover was the key to my happiness.

WHAT I LEARNED BEING SINGLE—AND WHAT I DIDN'T LEARN

In the early 1970s, hooking up on the first date was as common as shaking hands, and yet it wasn't working for me because I was still living by my old default belief systems. My therapist helped me become better attuned to the signals my dates were sending and the limitations of my thinking. This changed everything for me in terms of sexual intimacy, but internally it was a different story. I was still hiding my feelings of unworthiness, reinforced by the voice in my head with its never-ending self-criticism. I thought that any great woman would dump me if she knew how I felt inside.

Five years later, I was once again in a loving and faithful marriage to a beautiful woman. Eventually, after many more years of therapy, I learned that I wasn't emotionally defective; I was simply another human being with some insecurities, and I had nothing to hide. In hindsight I saw that up to that point I had built an elaborate strategy about feelings of don't ask, don't tell, which had kept me from true connection to myself and anyone else.

Since then, I've been able to reshape my thinking. Current neuroscience explains this in terms of our brain's malleability or neuroplasticity, which allows us to remodel our brains at any age, giving us the ability to think and act in new ways. Once I was no longer willing to stick to my don't ask/don't tell plan, my wife and I grew apart. Eventually the kids finished college and became independent, and we agreed to end the marriage.

FINALLY UNDERSTANDING WE NEED TO BE COMPLETE IN OURSELVES

When I entered the dating world again, the rules seemed to have changed back to the three-date waiting period to be sexually intimate (kind of like the three-day waiting period to buy a gun or get a high-interest loan). But for me the biggest changes occurred from learning about myself and the wisdom that comes with grey hair. I learned about *attachment longing*, which in my case came from an overly dramatic mother and the early death of my father, resulting in what felt like a bottomless longing for the right romantic attachment that would make me feel whole and complete.

Until I learned this, I'd thought that the right woman could fix things inside me as she did for Jack Nicholson's character in the movie *As Good as It Gets*, who says to his lover, "You make me want to be a better man." Today I understand that I'm the only one who can fill my need for attachment and love.

As I've discussed, a great deal of how we operate is due to the uniqueness of how we are wired and programmed psychologically and emotionally. For example, some of us are wired and programmed to have practical intelligence, and may have little or no emotional intelligence and others are wired and programmed to have emotional intelligence and may have little or no practical intelligence. Some of us are wired and programmed to be impulsive and to say or do things we later regret, and others are wired and programmed to deliberate about what we are going to say or do, sometimes for so long that we don't act at all and later regret not acting.

FULL SELF-EXPRESSION IS THE KEY

Today my new ability to be fully self-expressed has freed me from the solitary confinement that comes from living in a don't ask, don't tell world.

Now my greatest excitement is when I'm with someone whose wiring is complementary to mine, resulting in a true and free-flowing connection between us. Now I understand that good sex doesn't occur in the body, it lives in our minds, and that the only thing that matters to me is the exchange of energy generated from living a life of integrity and compatibility. For me, this means that if a woman is curious, playful, and empathetic and has a sense of adventure and a love of the spirit, which comes from introspection and personal growth, anything is possible.

Letting go of my old default positions has allowed me an inner peace that creates fearlessness, which, in turn, creates power and possibility. Now I am truly enjoying the best part of my life.

26

WHY I LOVE MY DOGS

I've always loved dogs. I had a couple of puppies when I was a kid, but they didn't last long. It always ended in mystery with my parents saying the puppy ran away. As a grownup, I got my first dog at twenty-four, to complete the family picture, and I've had dogs ever since.

Right now I have two dogs, Free Spirit and Charlie. Both dogs are big and incredibly fluffy, and they are constantly looking for food and love. I have never seen an aggressive action from either of them. We get along fantastically. Finally someone to get along with and whom I can make happy!

HOW DOGS DIFFER FROM PEOPLE

Here are my thoughts about why it's so simple to get along with dogs:

When I became aware that the voice in my head was the product of my mind's judgments and interpretations and, therefore, wasn't always telling me the truth, I started to listen to other people in a new way: I started listening at the level of *subtext*, the emotions and objectives underlying the words.

I first learned about subtext when I studied acting. I learned that "It's never just the words, but it's always the subtext." The words change meaning depending on the actor's objective and intention and the emotional resonance the words are imbued with as a result of what the character wants and does.

Scene 1: Let's say you're watching a scene in which a woman points a gun at her man and says, "I love you so much," and you know she's going to shoot because she's jealous and thinks he betrayed her.

Scene 2: Same actress and the exact same words, but this time she's seducing the guy. Now when she says "I love you so much"— the same words—it has a whole different subtext.

As I became more mindful, I stopped listening to just the words and listened instead at what was happening on an emotional level (the subtext). Today I work to experience people at the level of their machinery or how they are wired and programmed. Take the example I used earlier of being with a child who is having a terrible tantrum. At first you might think this is a poorly behaved child who probably has never had good parenting, but if a moment later you learn that the child is autistic, you have empathy for the child, knowing it's his wiring and not poor parenting that causes this behavior, so you're okay with it even if it's uncomfortable.

Another example is when I'm doing business with someone who just won't stop bargaining. I understand that her wiring is such that she just has to win, so I let her win on little things to keep the relationship workable.

It's the same when someone I know is shy and introverted and can't look me in the eye. Now I understand this behavior at the level of that person's machinery, and I can be loving without getting much back emotionally because I understand that's just how he or she is.

It's also the same with a woman who flirts with everybody and needs a response from all the men in a room. I don't take it personally because I can see that her machinery makes her like a bee pollinating flowers; she is wired and programmed to make her flirtatious.

What does this have to do with dogs? There is no subtext with dogs.

UNCONDITIONAL LOVE

I believe we human beings have a built-in Wi-Fi system that is always searching for similarly wired and programmed systems (people). This is part of how our brains work. For each of us, this system's effectiveness is closely related to how attuned we are to ourselves and to the messages others send us—in other words, how well both our individual Wi-Fi and our curiosity systems work.

My Wi-Fi system picks up the dogs' unconditional love without any complications. No matter what time I wake up, the dogs are patiently waiting to greet me with licking and wagging tails. If that isn't love, what is it?

The very presence of the dogs is comforting to me. They bring warmth. It's like having an air purifier—the dogs are a vibe purifier. It's like having a scented candle in the room.

Dogs don't want jewelry. They don't get an allowance. And the absolute worst thing that mine do is making a mess in the house. Dealing with that doesn't take a marriage counselor or attorneys. It just takes plastic gloves and a trash bag.

The dogs' Wi-Fi system has far fewer needs than mine. Their love comes in local color just like cartoons. Donald Duck is always white and his cap is always pure blue; dogs are always generating a pure love, and their needs are food and shelter and to be loved back.

If my dogs want to play and I don't have patience for it, they will love me just the same. Dogs make me feel safe and easy.

And I do love playing with my dogs, which often reminds me of how nice it was to play with my children when they were three and four years old, when I could easily make them laugh.

Pause Your Machinery

Relationships take work, and sometimes we forget that how we act in a relationship affects it as much as how the other person acts. Find a quiet place to think about your relationships as you do the following exercises.

- If you are in a long-term situation or relationship that you feel is like being a frog in hot water, describe the situation or relationship and what it feels like to be in it. Reflect mindfully on it, and describe the factors that are keeping you stuck.

  Can you identify a myth about yourself that is one of the factors that's keeping you there? If so, describe the myth. Describe why it's a myth and not the truth.

  Now reflect on the three choices you have about coping with it. Are you going to (1) accept the situation or relationship fully, warts and all, (2) change it, or (3) leave it?

  If you're going to accept it fully, describe the transformation in yourself and the steps you will take in your attitude to accept it fully. Formulate in words the Organizing Principles that have made you not accept it up to now and the new Guiding Principle that embodies your new attitude with which you can accept it.

  If you're going to change the relationship and situation, describe the transformation that you would like to take place in the relationship and the steps that you will take to transform it. Remember: tweaking what you've been doing up to now won't work to transform it; changing requires real transformation. What will you do differently from what you've done before? Is this a change you can make on your own, or do you need to engage at least one other person in making this change? Describe the steps you will take to engage the other person or people committing to changing it with you.

If you're going to leave the relationship or situation, describe the steps you will take to leave it. Include your willingness to risk the unknown, which means being willing to give up the familiar pain and experience the awkward pain of going into uncharted territory. Describe what you would like for yourself in the language of possibility.

- Reflect mindfully on whether you judge other people, either silently—keeping your judgments to yourself—or vocally—expressing them to the people you're judging. If you do judge others, describe what these judgments do to your relationships with the people you're judging.

  Reflect on why you have developed this habit. Describe the experiences in your past that led you to form this pattern of behavior.

  Describe what you get from judging others (does it make you feel superior, for example?). Describe what it costs you to judge others (does it create a distance between you and others, for example?).

  Reflect on whether this habit of judging others also shows up in judgments of yourself. If so, describe how it feels when you judge yourself.

  Now think about whether you're willing to let go of this pattern of behavior. Describe what steps you'll take to accomplish this and what you will do from now on when judgments pop into your mind, as undoubtedly they will.

- If you have a pet, just for fun, describe your pet and what you love about him or her.

Part V

MINDFULNESS AND WORK

27

WHEN WE ARE MINDFUL, WE ARE AT PEACE, AND WHEN WE ARE ON AUTOMATIC PILOT, WE CAN FEEL LIKE WE ARE IN A WAR ZONE

A few months ago I was in a significant negotiation meeting, and I reminded myself that I must let go of my attachment to my point of view, listen to what the other side is suggesting, and be open to possibility. In other words, I was telling myself to be mindful—to be in the here and now instead of creating an internal war zone by being on automatic pilot and carrying with me the baggage of the past.

We think we're making conscious decisions when we're on automatic pilot, but we are not experiencing what is actually happening here and now. Without realizing it, we are letting our default programming make choices, keeping us repeating our past in the present and carrying it into our future. This type of behavior is the opposite of mindful; it is *mindless*.

Indeed, Dan Siegel, MD, author of *The Mindful Brain: Reflection and Attunement in the Cultivation of Well-Being*, says that the "natural" state of the "unawakened mind" is to be mindless.[1] The bottom line is that running on automatic pilot creates unnecessary frustration, stress, and pain. And it limits us.

When we are mindless, our minds are filled with our judgments and interpretations of whatever situation we're in, so we never just experience the situation as it is.

When we are mindful, we experience each situation without being attached to past situations and past outcomes, and we are open to new possibilities. When we are mindful, we can be attuned to others, which makes resolving conflicts easier, whether in our personal relationships or our work relationships.

BEING OUR BEST SELF

It's helpful to remind ourselves that every situation is, in fact, a new situation. When we are mindful, we allow our higher self—the present, nonjudgmental, reflective, emotionally intelligent part of us—to be in the room; we bring our best self into the situation we are in and our old stories stop having power over us and thus stop bringing us into the past.

When we are mindful, we live in the moment; our entire experience is what's happening now, now, now as opposed to then, then, then. Our machinery is forced offstage in pause mode until we allow it to creep back onto center stage by becoming mindless again and allowing it to operate on automatic pilot.

We develop mindfulness by intentionally focusing in the now, exactly as it is.

WHY IT'S CRUCIAL TO BE IN THE NOW

The now is where things truly happen. All actions are executed in the present, the now. Completion is always in the now, experiencing what is occurring just as it is. Failure and success are not facts; they are just how the voice in our head judges what is occurring.

When we are mindful, our thoughts and fears won't paralyze us, our stories will dissolve, and we can just take care of business. When we stay mindful, we remember that success and failure are constructs of the machinery, and we know that in actuality there is no good or bad, there is just what's so.

Being mindful helped me to be effective in the negotiation meeting I mentioned because it helped me to be attuned to the other people, to hear their points of view, and to present my own without self-righteousness and despite fears I had about not being heard. It helped me to let go of any interpretation of winning or losing and to just be there in the present, open to possibility.

28

HOW MINDFULNESS CAN HELP US IF WE NEED TO CHANGE JOBS OR CAREERS

Changing careers out of choice can be challenging and can trigger fears; losing a job and needing to find a new one can be especially challenging and almost inevitably triggers fears. This is when mindfulness is vital.

The first step we can take to cope with fears and move ahead is to mindfully remind ourselves that both the voice in our head and the identity that it has crafted for us are only parts of who we are—forceful parts, but just parts. The mind's machinery doesn't want this secret to be revealed; it doesn't want us to know, "I have a choice whether to believe or not what the voice in my head is telling me. I don't have to allow the voice in my head to boss me around. And who I am is more than what I think of as my identity."

OUR JOB, OUR IDENTITY, AND OUR EMOTIONS

For many of us, our job and our money have become who we think we are, and losing a job and the financial security that may come with it can seem much the same as having who we are die. If we lose a job or our money, the voice in our head may tell us that we're a failure and make frightening projections about the future.

Elisabeth Kübler-Ross, a great pioneer in writing about death and dying, identified what she called the "five stages of grief" to explain what we go through when a physical death occurs.[1] I believe it's akin to what many of us go through with the emotional trauma that comes from losing our job and financial security.

Kübler-Ross described the five stages as denial, anger, bargaining, depression, and acceptance. She said that when we lose a person close to us, until we go through these stages, we will not be able to let go of our old identity nor will we be able to experience the necessary rebirth of a new identity.[2]

ACKNOWLEDGING OUR FEAR AND MOVING AHEAD ANYWAY

Part of the emotions we experience with the loss of a job is our fear of change. This is why, as I've discussed, our mind's programming would rather have us stay in a painful place that our minds are familiar with and that we know we can live with than to change and risk unknown pain. (This is familiar pain versus awkward pain, where we unconsciously feel that the current painful situation is better than what may await us in an unknown future situation.)

When we are dominated by the fear of embarking on something new, we will be paralyzed.

Mindfulness empowers us to act in the most productive ways possible, even in challenging situations. If we can allow ourselves to experience and go through the emotions associated with the five stages of grief, we can act in a mindful way despite our fear; with mindfulness, we will be able to let go of the judgments and interpretations that the voice in our head may make—its stories about success and failure—and we can go into uncharted territory and find possibilities that allow us to create ourselves anew.

29

MENTORING

I was fifteen when I got a job working as an usher at the Beverly Movie Theatre in Beverly Hills. My boss, Myron, the theatre manager, looked and acted like Tony Soprano on *The Sopranos*. One day I came into his office with what he must have thought of as a stupid kid's question, and he told me, "Man up. Stop acting like a kid who's caught his dick in his zipper, and take care of business."

Myron didn't know it, but he was one of my fist mentors. That crude and direct manly man talk brought me into a man's world. It meant "grow up or get out" and it catapulted me from Mr. Rogers's neighborhood to the jungle of the workplace.

I was shocked by the direct, without-sugar-coating way he talked to me, but instinctively I knew he was mentoring me, and I took his in-your-face advice to heart.

MY INTRODUCTION TO BEING A MENTOR

I was in my forties going through the hurricane of blended family chaos when Miriam Solomon, PhD, a wonderful therapist, introduced me to the concept of mentoring others as a way to work out the parenting skills that had eluded me.

Dr. Solomon explained that there comes a time when most boys need to separate from being their father's child to being his peer as a man; this usually comes with a kind of drama. I missed out on that experience with my dad because of his early death when I was a child.

Dr. Solomon suggested that I start mentoring young people because mentoring relationships are parentlike relationships in that the mentor is being supportive of other people and giving them guidance but without the complex issues that parenting involves.

ASKING PEOPLE WHAT THEY WANT OUT OF LIFE

I'm grateful for Dr. Solomon's advice. As a mentor, I contribute to younger people's lives by sharing life lessons I've learned professionally and personally. The people I mentor are generally in their late twenties or thirties.

Typically they ask me, "How did you do it?" And I will ask, "Do what?" Almost invariably I find from their answers that they think success is the prize and it's measured by money and the material symbols that come with it.

I usually set that aside and ask the mentee, "What is your goal in life?"

This is where the life lessons generally start to develop. Most of the young people I mentor see their journey as finding a way to be rich; I try to bring the conversation into practical reality. I ask questions like, "When you're fifty, what do you want your life to look like?" I ask them specific questions such as the following:

"Do you want a family?"

"If you do, how many kids do you want?"

"Where do you want to live?"

"How big a house do you want?"

"How many hours a day do you want to work?"

Their answers usually lead to more questions like, "Do you want your children to go to private or public school?" and "What do you want your vacations to look like?"

We'll start speculating on what their life will look like if they pursue the goals they've described, and I start to focus on what that lifestyle would cost. I ask them, "Do you think you'll be able to make that amount of money?" I also ask the most important question: "Is that lifestyle what you really want, with all the work and responsibility that come with it?"

I talk about what they would have to do professionally to earn the money needed to support what they tell me is the lifestyle they want. I explain the kind of working life that is generally associated with that level of career and ask, "Do you want to work twenty-four hours a day?"

We talk about the emotional cost of living the professional life necessary to get their picture of a celebrity lifestyle, and the picture becomes far less glowing to them. Then I bring the conversation around to talking about quality of life, which is what I believe truly brings happiness.

WHAT DO WE REALLY VALUE MOST?

When I started building my business, I thought money was the answer to everything, and I was willing to do whatever it took to get it. Back then I was in my early twenties, and I had no understanding of my inner world, let alone the inner worlds of other people. It wasn't until I was in my thirties that I embarked on the search for what really brings inner contentment.

I've noticed an amazing phenomenon: many young people have chosen career paths that are actually counter to what they really want.

When I was their age, I had no idea that eventually I would be an artist and a writer. In hindsight, I would have enjoyed an artist's life, but I'd never been exposed to it and had no idea it was a part of who I really am. I ask the people I mentor about their desire for creative expression and if the professional trajectory they're on is going to take them to a place of inner contentment.

BEING AUTHENTIC AND ALIGNING GOALS AND EXPECTATIONS

I believe that the primary life lesson is to be your authentic self in order to have a fulfilling life. The authentic you is not just the image you think you should show to the world. It's not who you think you should be because others expect it of you or because you expect it of yourself. The authentic you is who you truly are emotionally and temperamentally and the collection of your actual interests and needs as a whole person. This is the you that must be fulfilled in order to arrive at a life of inner contentment.

A concept that's especially helpful for me as a mentor is talking about goals and expectations. I'll ask, "What is your dream car?" Then I'll ask, "What do you think will be the best car you'll ever own?" If, for example, they say their dream car is a Ferrari but they think the best car they'll ever own is a Toyota, I explain that we generally get our expectations but miss our goals unless our goals and expectations are the same.

The major issues I focus on are (1) examining the cost of the lifestyle my mentees say they want, (2) aligning their professional goals with their expectations, and (3) determining whether the lifestyle they say they want is the one they really want.

For example, it's widely known that the top professional jobs often start out with a sixty-to-seventy-hour workweek that takes precedence over one's personal life, and for someone to succeed as a top professional, it will probably stay that way for the next twenty years.

I ask mentees, "Are you willing to pay that price?" Often the response I get is a blank expression of shock. The wind is knocked out of their sails. This is when I start guiding them to redefine their goals and align them with their expectations, and I take pleasure in knowing that I am playing a part in helping them chart a realistic path to their future. I also help chart a path for those who want to work sixty to seventy hours for twenty years to accomplish their goals, and this is rewarding, too.

Mentoring is, indeed, a gratifying experience that shares many aspects with parenting and, as Dr. Solomon told me, helps to develop parenting skills. I recommend it to anyone who feels a desire to share his or her professional experience and insights to contribute to the lives of others. And for anyone starting a career, building a career, or at a critical crossroads in a career, I recommend finding the right mentor.

Pause Your Machinery

The following exercises will help you approach situations mindfully.

- Reflect mindfully on recent situations at work in which you experienced stress and frustration. Describe the parts of your programming that caused you to respond in these situations as you did. Describe the Organizing Principles that you allowed to run you. Describe how they created stress and frustration for you.

  Reflect on how you could have approached these situations mindfully. Write the Guiding Principles that would have helped you respond to the situation mindfully. Keep these Guiding Principles handy and refer to them next time you're in a work situation that has the potential to activate your default programming so you'll stay mindful and decrease your stress and frustration and increase your effectiveness.
- Reflect on how you can use mindfulness if you are feeling trapped, have lost your job, or want to change jobs or careers. Identify and describe the Organizing Principles that keep you in the past and pose obstacles to your being in the present and approaching your situation from the perspective of possibility. Write new Guiding Principles to replace these dysfunctional Organizing Principles. Describe the steps you will take to apply these Guiding Principles to support you in achieving the goal you set for yourself.
- Write a list of people you know who you believe might be a good mentor for you. Write down the areas in

which you would like mentoring and any specific questions you may have. You can use this information to give the person an idea of your needs as a mentee.

I highly recommend being open to being a mentor. The rewards for you can be as great as the rewards for your mentee.

Part VI

TOOLS FOR SELF-TRANSFORMATION

30

BENEFITS OF KEEPING A JOURNAL—PART 1

I've kept a journal (or diary) for the last thirty-three years. I started in my midthirties. At that point, I'd been in therapy for five years, during which time I'd gotten the emotional strength to deal with my first marriage. Both my first wife and I were much too young (twenty-one and twenty-two) and immature when we married, and after nine years we were both very unhappy.

The first year of therapy centered on identifying my true issues that were causing me to be unhappy. In the process, I came to learn why my marriage was not going well, and therapy helped give me the ability to see and actualize a separation and divorce. During the next four years, I met, courted, and married my second wife. By the time I remarried, I thought I'd grown a lot through therapy and that it was time to quit.

By then, I'd gotten used to having the sympathetic listening of my therapist, I understood how important it was for me to be able to download to someone, and I decided that the journal would be my new listener.

I liked keeping a journal and have never stopped. Even though I started therapy again, I write in my journal every day. I now see that the first fifteen years were filled with references of me describing how I felt like a victim in some of my closest relationships. Journal writing was certainly a better choice than badmouthing, criticizing, or complaining to whoever would listen. I was still repeating the pattern of whining without doing anything about it.

HOW JOURNALING HELPED ME TO ACT MINDFULLY INSTEAD OF JUST WHINING

Once I recognized this, I began looking at journal writing in a different way: to reflect on what I've written and, if I'm complaining, see what I want to do about it. This has resulted in a great benefit. After I've written the same complaints a few times, I get clear about my problem and my reluctance to truly deal with it, and I remember that there are always the same three options for any situation I'm unhappy with. I can accept the situation fully, change the situation, or remove myself from the situation.

All of us have the ability to learn about our psychological and emotional makeup and to change if we have the motivation to do so.

A few days ago, I ran into an old friend who is the chancellor of a large school for therapists, and he told me a joke. The setup was a question: "How many therapists does it take to change a light bulb?" The punch line was "One . . . if the light bulb is truly ready to be changed."

OUR BRAIN AND SELF-TRANSFORMATION

Part of what has supported me in being ready to change habits—the kinds of habitual behavior I've found myself writing about in my journal—is what I've learned about neuroscientists' new findings about the brain.

All of us are born with similar components of our central nervous system, which includes our brain and the neural circuitry throughout our body. As I've discussed, the wiring and signal system for each of us is always similar yet also unique, just like our fingerprints. It's this unique wiring of our brain and the rest of our central nervous system that makes us think and act in different ways.

Scientists tell us that we are born with over 100 billion neurons in our brain. Over time, starting in our infancy, these neurons organize themselves to create who we become psychologically, emotionally, and biologically as we interact with the world. Many in the scientific community believe this process of development lasts long after adolescence. I personally believe the process continues throughout our lives into old age. The malleability of our brain means that as we use our minds mindfully instead of on automatic pilot, our brain can actually develop new neural pathways. Thus the process of self-transformation actually transforms our brain.

A GREAT AHA

I had a great aha when through mindfully reflecting on what I was writing in my journal, I finally got that my whining or complaining was never really about another person but was really about my own unfulfilled expectations.

I realized that every unfilled expectation is due to a story I made up about whatever it is that happened. When we think that someone is wrong for the way he or she treats us, it's because we're telling ourselves a story that justifies our belief that

that person should be the way we expect or want that person to be instead of the way he or she is.

We all believe our story is the only true story and that the other person should think and act as we do. It's human nature for most of us to understand intellectually that these stories cause us to react as we do, but most of us leave it at that—as a kind of abstract thought—and still keep getting upset. It's similar to how a cigarette smoker reads the smoking-causes-cancer warning on a pack of cigarettes and smokes anyway—unless and until the smoker finally gets and owns the truth of the warning and stops smoking.

LETTING GO OF A SELF-DEFEATING HABIT

When I finally owned that another person isn't wrong to act differently than I expect or want, I felt no need to complain and whine anymore. I recognized that the other person was just coming from his or her unique truth, which was assembled by that person's unique wiring and with unique operating principles based on his or her unique life experience.

I came to see, as I've discussed, that the other person's wiring is just different from mine, and that that person is the perfect version of who he or she is (no matter how much I want the person to be different), just as I am the perfect version of who I am. Indeed, we all think and act uniquely as a result of our unique wiring.

When we believe our story is the only true story, we fail to be mindfully aware of the differences between our wiring and other people's wiring. Whining about these differences and the hurt feelings that come from our unfulfilled expectations isn't going to do any good. Our job is to observe what is actually going on as opposed to the story we are making up and to figure out how to accept what's happening fully, negotiate a satisfactory resolution with other people, or walk away.

Now whenever I find myself starting to whine in my journal about a recurring issue, I ask myself if this is another example of me doing the same thing over and over and expecting a different result—the definition of insanity. Keeping a journal has helped me notice my whining and, gradually, to acknowledge and accept people's uniqueness—and this has enriched my life.

31

BENEFITS OF KEEPING A JOURNAL—PART 2

Every time I have an insight I record it in my journal. When I find some of these have special importance, I place them in a file I call my Wisdom Pages. When I'm in a difficult or confusing situation, I refer to my Wisdom Pages and always find the answers to help me deal with the situation in a mindful, productive way.

I keep a daily reminder on my digital calendar—kind of like a sticky note on the refrigerator door—to remind myself: "Stop working to assure yourself that you are okay, lovable, special. Allow yourself to be angry when you're angry; your anger is legitimate and alive, and it needs to be expressed. When you stop hiding from it, you will heal. Until you touch/hold these feelings, you're stuck in shame."

IT ALL DEPENDS ON YOUR PERSPECTIVE

Another important lesson I remind myself of is that everything depends on the way I look at or hold it. As I've mentioned, I've come to see that each of us lives in our unique virtual world of perceptions (literally our own virtual reality); an equally important understanding is that we can instantly flip the way we see an experience—the way we see the world—by looking at it with another possible interpretation.

Here is a visual example: You can see the picture below as a profile of a candlestick or, if you flip your perspective, as two people in profile looking at each other.

It's hard to believe, but everything can be looked at from

this flipping perspective. For example, you might tell a runner she has to be careful she's running on an appropriate surface because running on a hard surface can cause knee damage. One person could interpret your comment as helpful information while another could interpret it as a criticism, as if you're saying that she is "wrong" or even stupid to be running on concrete.

It all depends on how the person hears or interprets what you're saying—and that person can flip it one way or the other. It's important to be mindful and realize that the eye can only see and the ear can only hear what the mind is willing to process; how we respond to every situation we encounter is dependent on our perceptions. The more mindful we are, the more accurately we experience the world.

FEELINGS ARE NOT FACTS

We often tend to see our perceptions as facts even though they are just our interpretations. That's why one of the most valuable lessons I've ever learned, which appears in my journal year after year and has a place of honor in my Wisdom Pages, is "Feelings are not facts." We may feel that something is the truth and that if someone doesn't feel as we do, he or she is wrong. But when this happens, it's just two different perceptions from two unique virtual worlds. And every virtual world can be flipped.

It's enlightening to consider the old adage that tells us to walk a mile in another's shoes. It really opens up our horizons for empathy, compassion, and the potential to resolve disagreements.

32

WHY I RECOMMEND MEDITATION

I meditated without realizing it for over forty years by running six miles, six days a week. I'd start running, and a minute into it I'd be in my runner's trance. The great thing about running was being unable to keep a focused train of thought on a subject even if I wanted to, so I experienced a free flow of thought, without the voice in my head grabbing any of the thoughts and ruminating on them. I now realize that my running experience was a form of the meditative process, which consists of not paying attention to (or shutting down) the constant chatter in our heads, thus allowing the mind to freely flow with whatever thoughts come up, without being attached to any of them.

HOW THE VOICE IN MY HEAD IS LIKE MY TWO DOGS

Today I do a mindful meditation practice in a peaceful room with my eyes closed. Sometimes, if I've forgotten to close the door, my dogs come in and nudge my arm so I'll pet them. I know they have a loving agenda, and yet they can take me out of the meditative state. My answer to this is to give them their chew toys to take their minds off me. It's a win-win for all of us.

When I begin my meditation, the voice in my head can be just like my dogs wanting my attention, chattering to me about that day's pebble-in-my-shoe problems. And like with my dogs, I have special tools—in this case, repeating my mantra and focusing on my breath—that occupy the voice in my head and help me to meditate.

Merriam-Webster Dictionary defines *mantra* as "a sound, word, or phrase that is repeated by someone who is praying or meditating."[1] I was given the word for my mantra by my meditation teacher, and I silently repeat that word to myself over and over during meditation to quiet my mind. I get the same effect of quieting my mind when I consciously focus on inhaling and exhaling.

Repeating my mantra and focusing on my breath are chew toys for my mind because they divert the energy and attention from the voice in my head, freeing my mind from holding on to pebble-in-my-shoe problems and opening me to experiencing a meditative state.

I now see that while I ran, the act of running—my feet moving and my mind being occupied by constantly scanning the path in front of me so I wouldn't fall or run into anything—was also a chew toy for my mind that opened me to a more expansive state and created a feeling of well-being and peace.

THE REWARDS OF MEDITATION

The biggest reward from my meditation practice comes from an expanded mental state that is similar to dreaming even though I'm awake. Dreaming while asleep allows our unconscious to actively work out the agendas of both our conscious and unconscious problems.

Meditating allows the same free flow of thoughts to pass through my mind, and although I'm conscious of the thoughts, I'm not trying to hold on to or control them. It's just like watching clouds float across the sky. I see this process as allowing the neural pathways in my brain to freely flow while I simply witness the inner dialogue and let it go.

THE PRACTICE OF MEDITATION

I find that meditating for twenty minutes twice a day has given me an inner tranquility that I would have no access to otherwise, which is the primary reason I recommend meditation to you. Researchers have reported that mindful meditation also increases mindfulness,[2] and this has been my experience. To find out more about meditation and to access free guided meditations, visit http://marc.ucla.edu/body.cfm, a website hosted by the UCLA Mindful Awareness Research Center, where I studied meditation.

Pause Your Machinery

You can now move ahead using all you've learned. The following activities will help you get started.

- Keep a journal for a week and see if you find it beneficial. You can write your entries in a notebook or a file on your computer. I recommend writing every night before you go to bed. It really doesn't matter what you write about. Try writing about significant events of the day and any lessons you've learned. If you've had an upsetting experience, describe it and write about why it was upsetting. Reflect on it mindfully and, in hindsight, observe whether you acted on automatic pilot, letting your default programming run you. If so, describe what you'll do next time to decrease stress and frustration and cope with such situations more effectively. At the end of the week, read over your entries and see if you'd like to continue keeping a journal.
- Create your own Wisdom Pages. Again, you can write them in a notebook or in a file on your computer. I recommend starting off your Wisdom Pages by recording all the new Guiding Principles you've created in the Pause Your Machinery exercises that preceded this one. Add to these the major lessons you've learned that you've written about in these exercises. Then go over the entries you made in your journal and add lessons you've recorded there.
- Meditate every day for a week. Set aside five or ten minutes once a day and build from there. Choose a quiet place where you will not be disturbed. At the end of the

week, mindfully reflect on the experience of meditating, evaluate its benefits, and see if you would like to continue meditating.

CONCLUSION: LIVING IN TODAY'S FAST-CHANGING WORLD

I was sitting at an outdoor café and I noticed a photographer taking pictures of the adjacent vacant store that had a For Lease sign in its window. The photographer said he was documenting the demise of the era of the video store in America's history because Blockbuster, the leader in the video-store industry, had just announced its decision to close its remaining locations.

I immediately flashed back to the 1960s and to Mildred, whom I hadn't thought of in thirty years. She was the official office manager and unofficial housemother for the photography company I worked at while putting myself through college. Mildred was already in her sixties back then, so she has been a blessed memory for at least a decade already.

Mildred was married to Jack, who was one of those first adapters, the kind of person who was quick to take up new trends. One day Jack told me he was going to open one of the first video stores. At the time, the whole idea of a video store sounded like a harebrained scheme that was too far ahead of its time.

It's decades later now and things have changed. The digital revolution has put video rentals in the same category as pay phones, one-hour photofinishing, and telegrams—all still exist but are no longer mainstream businesses.

There's a regular rhythm and flow to life and to business as well.

The first popular camera, made by Kodak, was introduced in 1900, and its format lasted about one hundred years, until suddenly you could take a picture with a digital camera that didn't need film—and then you didn't even need a camera; you could take a picture with a cell phone. The printing press was invented in the Far East in the eleventh century and in Europe in the fifteenth century. For hundreds of years people read only printed books and, eventually, newspapers and magazines, so for centuries it seemed as if the printed word on paper was the only way we would ever read books, newspapers, and magazines. Now, up to 50 percent of novels are sold as e-books, and newspapers and magazines all have content on the Internet while many magazines are produced exclusively online.

Just as videos were replaced by DVDs, now both have been replaced by downloads from the Internet, and we can watch films and television shows on our computers, cell phones, and tablets.

The Buddha said the cause of human suffering is attachment to desire. To me, attachment is part of being human, especially attachment to other human beings. If we lose someone close to us, it is natural and appropriate to mourn them, miss them, and hold them in our loving memory. But what about attachment and the way it affects how we respond to other kinds of changes?

Today the rate of change in all fields is unprecedented. Every day we seem to lose some old and familiar staple of our life while an endless parade of new things is appearing. It may be challenging not to be attached to what was and to adapt to what is and will be, but it's necessary.

Attachment to the old keeps us in the past, and we thrive when we live our lives with integrity and enjoy what life offers us in the moment. The way to do this is to live our lives mindfully and to realize that if we lapse into automatic pilot, the very next moment we can be mindful again. This is the most valuable lesson I've learned about life and the most important message that I'm sharing with you.

NOTES

CHAPTER 2

1. Jonah Lehrer, "The Forgetting Pill Erases Painful Memories Forever," *Wired*, February 17, 2012, http://www.wired.com/2012/02/ff_forgettingpill/.

CHAPTER 3

1. Leana Melat, PhD (Jungian therapist), interview by author, February 20, 2015.
2. Ibid.

CHAPTER 5

1. Leana Melat, PhD (Jungian therapist), interview by author, February 20, 2015.
2. Ibid. C. G. Jung writes about the dark side throughout his works. For more information about the dark side, see particularly C. G. Jung, *The Collected Works of C. G. Jung*, vol. 6, *Psychological Types*, (Princeton, NJ: Princeton University Press, 1971), and C. G. Jung, *The Collected Works of C. G. Jung*, vol. 9, pt. 2 *Archetypes and the Collective Unconscious* (Princeton, NJ: Princeton University Press, 1969).

CHAPTER 6

1. *Merriam-Webster Online*, s.v. "perfect," accessed March 18, 2014, http://www.merriam-webster.com/dictionary/perfect.

CHAPTER 9

1. *Webster's New World College Dictionary*, 4th ed., s.v. "possibility." accessed July 2, 2013, http://www.yourdictionary.com/possibility#websters.

CHAPTER 12

1. *Oxford Dictionaries Online*, s.v. "outlier," accessed May 1, 2014, http://www.oxforddictionaries.com/us/definition/american_english/outlier.

CHAPTER 15

1. Randy Pausch, *The Last Lecture* (New York: Hyperion, 2008).

CHAPTER 19

1. Leana Melat, PhD (Jungian therapist), interview by author, February 20, 2015.

CHAPTER 22

1. Steven J. Fogel with Mark Bruce Rosin, *My Mind Is Not Always My Friend: A Guide for How to Not Get in Your Own Way* (Los Angeles: Fresh River Press, 2010), 154.

CHAPTER 27

1. Daniel J. Siegel, MD, *The Mindful Brain: The Neurobiology of Well-Being* (Louisville, CO: Sounds True, 2008), CD-ROM, disc 3.

CHAPTER 28

1. Elisabeth Kübler-Ross and David Kessler, "The Five Stages of Grief," www.Grief.com, http://grief.com/the-five-stagers-of-grief/.
2. Ibid.

CHAPTER 32

1. *Merriam-Webster Online*, s.v. "mantra," accessed June 20, 2014, http://www.merriam-webster.com/dictionary/mantra.
2. Daniel J. Siegel, *The Mindful Brain: The Neurobiology of Well-Being* (Louisville, CO: Sounds True, 2008), CD-ROM, disc 1; and "Benefits of Mindfulness," Helpguide.org, www.helpguide.org/harvard/benefits-of-mindfulness.htm.

INDEX

ABOUT THE AUTHOR

Steven J. Fogel has been described as a "Renaissance man for the new millennium." He is a cofounder of Westwood Financial Corp., one of the leading private commercial real estate owners in the country. For decades he has been an active participant in the human potential movement, inspiring and mentoring others to seek their true selves. As a longtime student of human behavior and development, he has studied with psychologists, educators, and rabbinical scholars. Steve is an accomplished artist and the author of *Your Mind Is What Your Brain Does for a Living*, published by Greenleaf Book Group Press; *My Mind Is Not My Friend: A Guide for How Not to Get in Your Own Way*, published by Fresh River Press; and *The Yes-I-Can Guide to Mastering Real Estate*, published by Random House. His broad experience in business and the arts led him to serve as chairman of the California Arts Council. He lives and works in Los Angeles.

Steve would love to hear from you. Let him know if these insights and personal stories have been helpful, and if you have insights that could be helpful to others. Contact Steve via:

e-mail: stevenjayfogel@gmail.com

Facebook: www.facebook.com/StevenJayFogel

Twitter: @stevenjfogel

Goodreads: www.goodreads.com/stevenjayfogel